READ!
READ!
READ!

Laurie Glass | Linda Peist | Beth Pike

READ!
READ!
READ!

Training
Effective
Reading
Partners

CORWIN PRESS, INC.
A Sage Publications Company
Thousand Oaks, California

For information:

Corwin Press, Inc.
A Sage Publications Company
2455 Teller Road
Thousand Oaks, California 91320
E-mail: order@corwinpress.com

Sage Publications Ltd.
6 Bonhill Street
London EC2A 4PU
United Kingdom

Sage Publications India Pvt. Ltd.
M-32 Market
Greater Kailash I
New Delhi 110 048 India

Printed in the United States of America

Library of Congress Cataloging-in-Publication Data

Glass, Laurie
    Read! read! read!: Training effective reading partners / by Laurie
Glass, Linda Peist, Beth Pike.
        p. cm.
    Includes bibliographical references and index.
    ISBN 0-7619-7634-5 (cloth: acid-free paper)
    ISBN 0-7619-7635-3 (pbk.: acid-free paper)
    1. Reading—Parent participation—United States—Case studies.
2. Books Pals (Program) 3. Home and school—United States—Case studies.
I. Pike, Beth.   II. Peist, Linda.   III. Title.
LB1050.2 .G54 2000
372.42′5—dc21

99-050598

This book is printed on acid-free paper.

00   01   02   03   04   05   10   9   8   7   6   5   4   3   2   1

Corwin Editorial Assistant: Julia Parnell
Production Editor: Denise Santoyo
Editorial Assistant: Cindy Bear
Typesetter: Rebecca Evans
Cover Designer: Oscar Desierto

Contents

Preface

Our program, "Book Pals," was created to address a need among educators to more effectively involve parents in the process of helping their children learn to read and write. Although at-risk readers are provided with supplemental support at school, additional reinforcement is needed from home to maximize children's learning potential. While much has been written about how parents should read aloud to their children, little has addressed how teaching parents to be effective reading partners can substantially improve their children's literacy achievements. This book goes beyond other publications by supplying the educator with a structured program that trains parents to implement a variety of techniques. Parents are afforded an opportunity to truly participate in their children's literacy development because they are given knowledge of the reading process and helped to understand their invaluable role.

Read! Read! Read! provides a framework of concrete information that will guide educators in the most successful way to involve and train parents. We supply the background knowledge and tools professionals will need to run their own series of parent workshops. Included is a reproducible parent guide that contains information to be distributed to parents as a supplement to the workshops.

Specific workshop agendas and all supporting information facilitators will use are presented in a manner easily adaptable for the specific needs of various educational situations. The content of our book can be used by a broad spectrum of individuals. This includes primary educators, special education teachers, reading specialists, Reading Recovery™ leaders and teachers, curriculum supervisors, principals, education majors in college, parents who homeschool, and anyone else who wants to learn how to successfully integrate parents into the development of children's literacy. The tools necessary to foster positive communication between home and school is included. Information is presented in a reader-friendly manner, making it easy for workshop facilitators to use.

Even educators who have no intention of facilitating the workshops will find the extensive amount of information regarding the development of literacy valuable when teaching their students, collaborating with colleagues, and communicating with parents regarding their children's reading and writing progress.

Parents who are interested in expanding their knowledge regarding their own children's literacy will benefit from the running glossary that clearly explains technical terms. The reproducible parent guide clearly outlines the techniques parents can use when their children are learning to read and write.

The book is organized in a concise manner, with each chapter self-contained in terms of the concepts and topics discussed. Knowledge can be gained from reading the book in its entirety or choosing those chapters of particular interest.

Chapter 1 discusses why the program was created and describes how the series of workshops trains parents to become effective reading partners with their children. Major concerns parents have expressed regarding their children's reading are addressed. Benefits of the workshops and the importance of a supportive home environment are also included.

Chapter 2 is highlighted by a sequential description of book levels and reading stages, expectations for the reader at each level, and how parents can offer support. Information provided shows the importance of allowing children to progress at their own pace and how strategies at each stage are cumulative and must be built upon. The developmental stages are described using sample dialogue between a student and teacher during reading.

Chapter 3 addresses the issue of phonics as one strategy readers are taught to use in figuring out unfamiliar words. Information is provided on how parents can help their children develop phonemic awareness through poems, activities, and games. Included in the chapter are explanations and activities focused around onsets and rimes and multisyllabic words as a key to fostering independent word attack skills. Educators are provided with additional sources for games and activities.

Chapter 4 discusses the various ways children can demonstrate their comprehension skills. Responding through discussion and writing is broken down into components showing how children are invited to participate in the reading process. Frequently asked questions by parents regarding their children's writing are addressed.

Chapter 5 presents our model for facilitating the four workshops. The first part of the chapter answers questions regarding the practical considerations when preplanning, including attendance, location, and equipment. Four sample agendas are then offered with specific activities and details.

Chapter 6 includes questions and answers about conducting the workshops. We suggest alternative ways to implement workshops based on the facilitators individual needs and target audience. An e-mail address is available for questions by the reader.

Chapter 7 discusses how the workshops respond to the needs of the more disabled reader. We suggest various ways to expand our techniques to help children capitalize on their strengths and compensate for their weaknesses.

We share creative and multisensory activities that allow these children to develop more independence in their reading.

The reproducible Parent Resource Guide is user-friendly and meant to be used in its entirety as a supplement to the parent workshops. It is based on our own program, "Book Pals," which we currently use in our schools. Facilitators can also distribute sections of the guide that are applicable to their needs. Simple terminology is used so the material is easily understood by parents. Prompts, praise, and a positive environment are stressed as vital to children's literacy success.

Acknowledgments

The contributions of the following reviewers are gratefully acknowledged:

Ken Schatmeyer
Director of Curriculum (K-12)
Southeast Local School District
Wooster, Ohio

Cris Riedel
School Library Media Specialist
Ellis B. Hyde Elementary School
Dansville, NY

Octavio Furtado
Assistant to the Superintendent
Randolph Public Schools
Randolph, MA

Lois Spregnether
Head of Children's Services
Mount Clemens Public Library
Mount Clemens, MI

Special thanks to our principal, Jacqueline Martin, for supporting the implementation of the workshops and for creating a working environment that encourages parent involvement and creativity.

Our appreciation to Mary Jean Hart for sharing her Reading Recovery™ expertise and being there from the beginning.

We would like to thank the entire Milford Brook staff for making children's literacy a priority.

Our appreciation to all the workshop parents who not only participate in the program but have dedicated themselves to making a difference in their children's lives.

We would also like to thank Jay Whitney, Denise Santoyo, and Kelly Gunther for their support and help with this book.

To Sara for leading us in the right direction.

Thanks to David Jay for his legal expertise.

We gratefully acknowledge the contribution of the NJEA Frederick L. Hipp Foundation for Excellence in Education, Inc.

—Laurie Glass, Linda Peist, and Beth Pike

To my family and friends for their enthusiasm and encouragement in everything I do. Thanks to my mom, Jean, for providing all those home-cooked meals and to my dad, Marty, for his great accounting advice. To Michael, Barbara, Mark, and Jessica, thanks for being a part of my life. My gratitude to Fred Smith and the kids at Camp Daisy for inspiring me to become a teacher.

—Laurie Glass

I would like to thank my family for their support. To my parents, Fannie and Francis Crosett, I will always be grateful for encouraging me to teach. Special thanks for my husband, Rob, for his love and patience while writing the book and for the time we spend over morning coffee. To my daughter, Suzanne, I am especially thankful for your computer knowledge and your willingness to help the technologically challenged. For my son, Dave, whose sense of humor always makes me laugh. I love you all very much.

—Linda Peist

To my mother, Blossom, who always made me feel whatever I did was wonderful. She is greatly missed. To my father, Bernie, and Susan for always supplying encouraging words and love. To Aaron for his great cooking and support. To Alan, Karen, and the gang for all their company. To Tom for his love and understanding when vacations were not possible. To my daughter Jodi for being so responsible, loving, and encouraging, and to my daughter Rena for sharing her room and computer with three temperature nuts, as well as her love, individuality, and good humor when no dinner was on the table.

—Beth Pike

About the Authors

Laurie Glass has a master's degree in education in counseling from Rutgers University. She has taught special education in the Manalapan-Englishtown Regional School District for 10 years and currently teaches second- and third-grade resource support students reading and math. She has published in the *School Librarian's Journal* and has presented a workshop on reading at Brookdale College.

Linda Peist has a master's degree in elementary education and has earned a reading specialist certificate from Georgian Court College. She has taught grades 1 through 6 for 30 years in the Manalapan-Englishtown Regional School District and currently teaches reading in grades 2 and 3. She has participated in the mentor program for new teachers in her school.

Beth Pike has a master's degree in special education from C.W. Post. She earned her Learning Disabilities Teacher Consultant certificate from Georgian Court College. She is currently a learning consultant in the Manalapan-Englishtown Regional School District. She has also taught resource support students grades K through 6, with an emphasis on first-grade reading acquisition, for 10 years.

Beginnings

Why We Created This Book

Reading instruction has always been at the forefront of educational debates. There are numerous theories on the best way to educate children to become successful, lifelong readers. Most of these theories focus on how the teacher guides students' achievement. Left out of the equation until recently, though, was the role parents play in their child's academic success. Research has shown that parental help with reading was a better predictor of a child's reading success than was intelligence and that this effect was sustained across socioeconomic groups and was independent of the home language (Hewison & Tizard, 1980). Yet, in reality, parents are seldom expected to do more than help with homework or read aloud to their children. Although these practices have positive implications, many educators frequently underestimate the role parents should assume in their children's literacy development. When thinking about working with parents, teachers may be hesitant due to their own lack of experience, time involved, or previous negative interactions with parents. However, parents of young children, especially those struggling with learning to read, need to be involved in their children's education. Educators must take the initiative to improve communication and provide parents with the tools necessary to accelerate their children's progress.

The workshops grew out of our need as teachers to engage parents in their children's literacy development. Our support program consists of many components that parents were not aware of. We chose to inform parents of the components in our successful guided reading program. We needed them to be aware that we encouraged children's growth by using the following techniques:

- Identifying and helping at-risk readers as early as possible
- Providing students with extensive opportunities to read and write

- Teaching self-monitoring strategies for reading and writing that children learn to apply in new situations
- Supplying students with authentic literature at their appropriate reading level
- Individualizing instruction
- Developing phonemic awareness
- Monitoring and assessing children's progress daily
- Conferring regularly with the children's classroom teacher
- Promoting students self-esteem through clear and meaningful praise
- Sending home literature books for children to reread

It was this take-home literature component of our program that the workshops intended to support. Parents had been listening to their children read and write but we felt that with more communication and education we could enrich the quality of home support. We felt that children could be empowered to take responsibility for their own reading success and parents could be shown how to positively support the school program. Given the proper tools and support, most students do learn to read.

We wanted parents to do more than just passively listen to their children read to them. A review of 40 studies concurred, noting that parents just listening to their child's reading was not enough. This practice does not result in literacy gains, particularly for the at-risk reader, unless parents have received some training in specific procedures to assist their children during the reading sessions (Toomey, 1993). The message was clear: We needed to create training sessions for parents.

What Exactly Is Read! Read! Read!?

Read! Read! Read! is based on "Book Pals," a series of workshops we created to be presented by educators to train parents to become more effective reading partners for their children at the primary level. Our particular model is to hold four evening sessions with parents of struggling readers to disseminate information, demonstrate techniques, and have parents implement at home the procedures they have learned. The first two workshops are presented to parents and afford them an opportunity to learn from the facilitators how to best support their children's literacy development. The children are invited to the third and fourth workshops where parents and children, guided by educators, are able to put into practice what they have learned.

However, this is only one model in which educators can use the workshops to take the opportunity to enrich the home-school connection, and it need not be limited to dealing with parents of at-risk children. We first provide specific information on the different aspects of our model, and then suggest alternative ways to implement the program.

How Parental Concerns Influenced the Workshops

In planning what we intended to cover in the workshops, we relied on our years of teaching experience and the many interactions we have had with parents. As primary educators working with struggling readers and their parents, we had insights into their concerns that surfaced throughout the year. Parents of struggling readers were often frustrated while listening to their children reread the books brought home from school. These children required more time, repetition, and direction when learning than their peers. Often, students reported to us that their parents would do things like cook dinner or talk on the phone while they were reading aloud to them. What message did those children receive? They were being told that their reading had no value and was not important enough to listen to. We wanted to help parents understand that their children needed undivided attention from them in order to support their reading.

Parents felt isolated and inadequate in attempting to help their children read, not realizing that there were other families with similar concerns. We wanted to increase parent-teacher contact time in a different setting, providing a forum where parents could express their uncertainties. We felt that if we could involve the parents in learning more about reading and provide them with support, we could increase our students' prospects for success and eliminate potential frustrations. Listed below are some of the major concerns from parents that we realized would have to be addressed at the workshops.

Why Reread the Book at Home When It Has Already Been Read at School?

In our program, we have students take home appropriately leveled books to reread to their parents. These books have already been read and discussed with the teacher in school. Parents initially underestimate the importance of rereadings.

Rereading is a productive method for improving reading ability. For those children who have difficulty learning to read, rereadings are the most universally used remedial technique to help poor readers achieve reading skills (Samuels, 1997). Children benefit from this technique in a variety of ways. By interacting with a book more than once, children gain confidence in their ability to handle the text and it becomes easier and more enjoyable. As children become familiar with the vocabulary, they rely less on decoding and increase fluency. When word recognition becomes more automatic, children can spend additional time focusing on comprehension. For struggling readers to receive maximum benefit from rereading the text, they should be supported by trained adult guidance particularly at the early developmental levels. At these stages, readers need praise and prompts given by an attentive adult to foster good strategy usage.

My Child Is Just Memorizing the Book

Parents of emergent readers often expressed concern about their child memorizing the text after several readings. They felt that memorization meant their child was not really reading. Parents sometimes tested their child's knowledge of vocabulary by having them read the text backward. When the child could not read that way, the parent would say they did not really know the words and were not reading. Parents did not understand the complexity of the process and how their child was integrating a variety of strategies when reading. It had to be explained to parents that memorization is a first step in the process of learning to read. Initially, children use memorization to build a bank of sight words. As the reading material becomes harder, the use of more reading strategies supersedes the memorization technique.

What Are These Strategies
My Child Talks About Using?

Strategies are thoughts that readers use to get meaning from text and figure out unknown words. We teach children to be strategic readers, but most parents lack this knowledge of strategies and the developmental nature of reading. Although parents sincerely wished to help their children, they would inadvertently discourage them from using a strategy that had been learned. For example, parents might cover up story pictures although at school the child had been taught to use them as a clue to figuring out unknown words. It needed to be explained to parents that pictures are not just an added interest but are a fundamental part of beginning reading.

We often encountered parents who remembered reading instruction from years ago when it was isolated and skill driven. Parents recalled reading as a process of decoding and tended to focus on sounding-out strategies as a primary means of identifying unknown words (Routman, 1991). We teach children to use phonics as one of many strategies when figuring out unknown words in context. Reading is a complex process that entails more than simply learning sounds and words in isolation. Good readers integrate the meaning of text, the structure of language, and visual cues throughout the reading process (Clay, 1991).

These examples demonstrate that parents lacked the understanding of the developmental aspects of reading. These workshops afford educators the chance to include parents in their children's literacy development so that crucial opportunities for children to practice independence in reading are not being lost.

My Child Does Not Seem to Be Able to Answer the Questions I Ask About the Story

The importance of comprehension in the process of reading cannot be underestimated. Parents need to learn how they can support this aspect of reading, which is even more important than decoding. We have found in the past that parents are perplexed by dealing with comprehension and frequently resort to asking literal questions. Some children may appear not to be comprehending because small details have been forgotten. For example, parents complain that their child does not understand what has been read when they are unable to answer a question such as, "What color was the boy's shoe?" In actuality, the child often understands the main idea and can make inferences about the story, thus making forgetting a minor detail not important in the overall process. It is frequently difficult for parents to grasp what constitutes good comprehension.

Parents must be trained how to ask meaningful, challenging questions rather than focusing on unimportant details. Good readers use factual information just to support inferences. Holdaway (1990) concurs noting that factual comprehension should be checked only when there has been a failure to achieve deeper understanding and as an exploration and diagnosis of that failure. One way to find the underlying meaning is to have parents and children relate what they read to personal experiences or previously read books.

We decided that after hearing these concerns year after year we would design a program to train parents on how to best support their children's literacy development at home. These workshops were initiated to provide this training to foster independence in reading.

Introducing the Workshops to Parents

We begin early in the school year to get parents involved in supporting their children's reading. It is important to start helping children as soon as possible, especially struggling readers. Our hope is to provide early intervention before the reading experience becomes negative. When our students take their first book home, it is accompanied with a letter explaining the rereading concept with suggestions on how to get the most out of the

Figure 1.1. Letter Sent to Parents at the Beginning of the School Year, Prior to the First Workshop

---

Fall, 2000

Dear Parents,

Throughout the year, your children will be bringing home books similar to the one enclosed in this reading folder to read to you. Most of the books should be read easily because we have read the story together in class. The purpose of rereading is to help children develop fluency and practice monitoring their own reading to be sure it makes sense. They will use strategies learned at school that will strengthen their self-confidence. Listening to your children read aloud is very important. Rereading is most successful when you:

Find a quiet time and place for the two of you to work. It is best if you sit side by side so you can both see the text. Your child should hold the book and be responsible for turning the pages.

Allow wait time (5 to 10 seconds) when your child encounters an unfamiliar word to try and figure it out independently. Your child will ask for help if needed.

If children misread a word and do not correct it, let them finish the sentence and then ask if the word makes sense.

Thank you for all your help,

**We invite you to our first meeting on September 25th at 7:00 p.m. in the school library. We will share techniques to help you become a more effective reading partner for your child. We look forward to explaining our reading program. We are confident that together we can make this a very successful year.

---

parent-child reading experience. The letter includes an invitation to the first of four workshops (see Figure 1.1).

We aggressively encourage parents to participate in the workshops by sending out flyers, making phone calls, and sending reminder notices through the mail. We are in the habit of talking "Book Pals" to our students so they begin to take ownership of the program and encourage their parents to attend the workshops. Children understand that this means they can read to an adult at home, like they do at school, and receive the same positive support.

It is crucial for parents to attend the first workshop. It provides an overview of the workshops and the vital role parents play in accelerating their children's reading progress. We talk about setting a positive atmosphere for reading together and explain the developmental stages of reading.

We also focus on what strategies good readers use to solve problems independently and the productive use of prompts and praise. We speak about comprehension and responding to literature both in conversation and in writing. We show a demonstration video that exemplifies the various aspects of reading we have discussed earlier in the meeting. The video we produced reflects several different stages of reading, modeling techniques used, and the positive interaction that should occur between the reader and the adult listener.

Benefits of the Workshops

The workshops provided a variety of benefits for parents and children that exceeded our expectations. Once parents understood how their children were being taught in school, they relaxed and were open to new ideas. We found a number of qualities that made workshops more inviting for parents.

Creating the Optimal Workshop Environment

From the beginning, we strive to establish a comfortable climate for parents. Primarily, they need to know their children are capable of learning to read and that they can be an important part of the process. We explicitly state that parental involvement boosts student achievement when done in a positive way.

Initially, parents are hesitant to discuss their own personal difficulties in working with their children at home. However, by the end of the first workshop they have relaxed enough to share their concerns with the whole group. The trust that develops opens up the lines of communication between not only the parents and facilitators but also the parents with other parents when they realize they share a common bond. For example, in a previous workshop, one parent expressed concern about finding time to read with their child when there were younger siblings at home. Other parents agreed that this was a problem, and they brainstormed to come up with solutions. These spontaneous interactions came to exemplify the team spirit that we were striving to achieve throughout the workshops.

We conclude all workshops with refreshments, and this has surprisingly developed into a significant component of the program. It has become an important time for parents to personally interact with the facilitators and each other in an informal atmosphere. Even though we address many aspects of reading and writing to the group, parents still need this time to relate what they have learned when working with their own children. We create an environment where parents feel comfortable enough to let their guards down and share their individual questions and concerns.

Using Parental Input to Direct Workshops

At the end of the first workshop, we distribute parent surveys to be returned at a later date. We seek parental input and use the responses to adapt the agenda for the next workshop. Incorporating parental input into the framework is one of the workshop's strengths. Although we approach each workshop with a set plan, we are aware of the value of having a flexible agenda. Each time workshops are held, we find the needs of the parents vary. As educators, we know the importance of making parents feel part of the process. We need to respect their concerns and value their input.

In past workshops, we noticed that many parents had major concerns about phonics in the reading process. They were either relying too heavily on sounding out or did not understand how to help their child use phonics at a developmentally appropriate level. We used their questions to direct the flow of the meeting. We found we needed to spend a substantial amount of time explaining the role of phonics in a balanced reading program.

Parents realize our sincerity when we actually incorporate their ideas in adapting our subsequent agendas. When parents attend future workshops, they come in prepared with questions and stories about techniques they have tried at home.

Parents occasionally bring up other issues during workshop discussions. Although these topics may not be directly related, they are of significant value. It speaks well of the rapport that develops between the workshop facilitators and parents that allows them to feel comfortable sharing other concerns. In helping parents find solutions to problems, we continue to build on the trust that has grown. A popular topic among parents is the amount and difficulty of their children's homework. Often, a homework assignment is inappropriate for an individual child's developmental reading level. We offer input into how the parent can discuss modifications of assignments with the classroom teacher in a positive and productive manner.

Tapping Parents for Information

There are additional reasons for increasing communication with parents besides discussing curriculum. When speaking with parents, they share valuable information that helps us view their children in another light. There are many benefits to these conversations, especially if the facilitator is also the child's teacher. First, the workshop affords parents the opportunity to speak proudly of their children's interests and accomplishments in areas other than reading. This is especially important for parents of struggling readers to help them accept their children's weaknesses and appreciate their strengths. Once they acknowledge the academic problem, parents become more open to accepting our suggestions for help.

Next, having personal knowledge of children's successes helps educators to specifically praise them and foster their interests. After learning from a parent that their child is interested in karate, the teacher could find books on the topic to read with her. This affords an opportunity to extend children's interests into writing as well. Children's strengths should be encouraged to increase their self-esteem and self-confidence. This also fosters a closer relationship between the teacher, parent, and student.

Conversations with parents also reflect insights into the importance literacy activities are given in the home and what goals the parents have for their children for now and in the future. When a positive relationship with parents is established, they are more willing to share medical and familial problems that may affect school performance. As they become more comfortable, parents are often willing to offer family history that may correlate to the child's reading problems. A parent could relate that a relative had dyslexia or trouble learning to read in school. In addition, the child may have had a specific problem, such as a lag in meeting their early developmental milestones or medical problems including a history of ear infections, which provides insight as to how the child's language matured.

Workshop facilitators should not underestimate the importance of informal discussions. Parents possess a wealth of information that can affect their children's learning that may have otherwise remained unknown to the facilitator.

Building a Positive Home Environment

At the first workshop, parents often share stories that reflect their frustration when monitoring their child's reading. One parent related that she was particularly upset when her son could read the word *the* on one page but not the next. She had threatened him with the loss of his birthday party if he did not read that word correctly. Other parents volunteered that they often got angry with their children and made similar types of threats even though they never intended to follow through. This was not done maliciously but rather out of the parents' frustration and lack of knowledge of how to help. Reading and writing at home had become something to dread for both parent and child. In contrast, these same children eagerly volunteered to participate in class where expectations were more realistic and difficulties understood. Parents did not realize the connection between the negative atmosphere they had unintentionally created and their children's lack of enthusiasm for reading with them.

These problems can lead to planned discussions on how to create the most supportive home environment when reading. We use a demonstration video of an adult and child reading together as a springboard to facilitate a discussion on how to set the proper tone at home.

After spending time discussing the aspects of a positive home environment, parents left the workshop with the skills to become more supportive reading partners. We begin the second workshop by talking about what techniques had been successful at home. Parents reported that the greatest change they noticed was in their relationship with their child during reading. The children responded positively to the praise, and support from their parents and reading at home became more pleasurable. Both parents and children were less tense. The readers were increasingly comfortable, taking independent risks, and were more likely to self-correct when their reading stopped making sense. Over time, children became better monitors of their own reading. They were eager to work when their parents expectations became more appropriate. We attributed this to the increased consistency of reading techniques between school and home.

Crucial Aspects of a Supportive Environment

The five major points listed below encompass our philosophy of creating a positive reading environment in which learning is more likely to occur. These points are used to educate parents on the basic requirements needed to be successful reading partners. Throughout our program, we continually refer to the necessity of incorporating these techniques into parent-child reading. We expect parents to come away from our workshops with the ability to apply these methods in the reading process.

1. *Find a quiet, comfortable place to read.* In establishing a quiet place to read, we suggest that parents find a space set apart from hectic daily activities. They need to make sure that siblings are engaged in other activities, away from the reading area, and will not interfere with the process. The parent and child should sit next to each other so they both can view the text. The child should hold the book and be responsible for turning the pages. We emphasize that reading should take place on a regular schedule when parents are not pressed for time. It should be a rewarding experience for both parents and children.

2. *Set realistic expectations for the child's progress.* We explain how unrealistic expectations can lead to disaster. Parents need to be made aware of the importance of text selection when reading. The books children are expected to read should be appropriate for the child's instructional level. We inform parents that children develop at their own pace and allowances have to be made for individual differences. Parents come to understand that they should not compare their child's rate of progress with a sibling or schoolmate. This is especially important for the parents of learning disabled

children who in many cases are progressing as fast as they can or may need adaptations in their program.

3. *Provide adequate wait time.* The issue of wait time must be clarified so parents realize the necessity of allowing their child opportunities to use reading strategies, and thus developing independence. Wait time is when the listener gives the reader time to attempt various strategies before providing assistance. If the listener helps too early they could be undermining the child's self-confidence. Children then believe that they can only be successful through the interventions of others, and feel incapable of making sense of their own mistakes. We explain that wait time is needed to allow a child to independently problem solve before prompts are given. Parents learn that readers need time to figure out unfamiliar words for themselves or to reread something when the meaning is unclear.

4. *Give specific praise when reading together.* Self-confidence is an extremely powerful motivator that helps children view themselves as successful readers. We explain to parents how important praise is in supporting their children's risk taking and self-monitoring. It is more meaningful when children know they have given their best effort and are respected and appreciated for trying. It is not sufficient to give vague comments, such as "Good job, Suzanne!" Instead, the praise needs to be sincere and specific reinforcing the child's use of strategies. The above comment could be altered to say, "Suzanne, I like the way you used the picture as a strategy and didn't immediately ask me for help." Specific praise allows children to understand what they are doing correctly and they are more likely to repeat that behavior. We stress that all comments need to be positive because the children are already aware that reading is difficult for them and they are not intentionally making mistakes.

5. *Offer timely prompts when the child is stuck on a word.* After a child attempts to independently figure out a word, the parent should always praise the effort. If the child's guess is wrong, then the parent needs to offer a helpful prompt. Prompts are specific phrases that encourage children's independence in problem solving when they are stuck in reading. For example, a good prompt might begin with a praise of the child's reading effort: "Rena, I like the way you tried to use the beginning sound to figure out that word." A specific prompt would then be given to encourage the child to use additional strategies: "Now Rena, let's reread the sentence to see if what you tried makes sense." Prompts will vary depending on the child's developmental reading level and independence. Additional examples of prompts and praise are available in the resource guide for parents provided at the end of this book.

Once parents attended the first workshop, they had committed to learning about their role in the reading process. They were eager to return for future workshops as evidenced by an attendance rate of more than 90% at all subsequent workshops. Parental responses on the questionnaires reflected their appreciation for the information and support they had received. Many commented that more frequent workshops would be helpful in maintaining their newfound skills. The three additional planned workshops were able to meet the parents' needs as well as providing the facilitators with the opportunity to see firsthand the interaction between parent and child.

This is how our workshops originated: educators and parents with a common goal, working as a team to improve children's reading at home and school. At subsequent workshops, we continue to provide parents with information they need to know to make their reading times increasingly productive. This gives parents a forum to continue to celebrate reading success and express new concerns as their role as listeners changes and their children's reading develops.

When we created the workshops, our expectation was to help parents become true reading partners with their children. Parents enthusiastically embraced the message in the first workshop, and emerged as part of our reading team. We had initiated a positive change, and the greatest beneficiaries were the children who were becoming confident, independent, lifelong readers.

References

Clay, M. (1991). *Becoming literate: The construction of inner control.* Portsmouth, NH: Heinemann.

Hewison, J., & Tizard, J. (1980). Parental involvement in reading attainment. *British Journal of Educational Psychology, 50,* 209-215.

Holdaway, D. (1990). *Independence in reading.* Aukland, New Zealand: Ashton Scholastic.

Routman, R. (1991). *Invitations: Changing as teachers and learners K-12.* Portsmouth, NH: Heinemann.

Samuels, S. J. (1997). The method of repeated readings. *The Reading Teacher, 50,* 376-381.

Toomey, D. (1993). Parents hearing their children read: A review. Rethinking the lessons of the Haringey Project. *Educational Research, 35,* 223-236.

The Developmental Aspects of Reading

C hildren's acquisition of reading strategies proceeds through a natural, sequential progression of stages not unlike those of children learning to walk. Each stage is equally important and must be built upon by the learner. Educators and parents working together can ensure continued progress by using techniques that are appropriate for each developmental stage. Children progress at their own pace and should not be rushed or compared with other children.

Reading Stages

Knowledge of the developmental nature of reading is crucial to teachers' and parents' abilities to support struggling readers in a meaningful way. Children progress along a continuum or ladder of strategies with the ultimate goal being independence in reading. *Strategies* are thoughts that readers use to get meaning from texts and figure out unknown words. For example, upon encountering an unknown word, a child might be taught to look at the pictures for clues, or use the beginning sound of a word to help figure it out. As children internalize a skill, it is added to their repertoire of strategies to be used when they are self-correcting their reading. The more diverse and extensive the set of strategies children develop, the better able they are to monitor their own reading in a variety of texts.

Listening to students read aloud is an excellent opportunity for educators to build on what they know about students' thinking. Educators can accurately assess which strategies children are able to use at any given time and base their instruction on what children need to learn.

Strategies—Thoughts readers use to get meaning from books to help them figure out unknown words.

Figure 2.1. Book Level Equivalence Chart

In our reading programs, we use literature books that are leveled based on the guidelines set by Reading Recovery™ . However, this program can be used with appropriate materials taken from many sources. We have created this guide so you can gage your materials accordingly.

Reading Strategy Stage	Approximate Reading Recovery™ Levels	Grade	Approximate Basal Series Levels
Emergent	1	Pre-kindergarten to Grade 1	Readiness
	2	Kindergarten to Grade 1	Readiness
	3,4	Grade 1	PP1
Beginning	5,6	Grade 1	PP2
	7,8	Grade 1	PP3
Transitional	9 through 13	Grade 1	Primer
Expanding	14 through 16	End of Grade 1	Grade 1
	17 through 20	Beginning Grade 2	Grade 2

Once children surpass the expanding stage, we rely on the more conventional levels like 2.5 to represent the middle of grade 2, and 3.1 and 3.5 for third-grade materials. The expectations for handling texts remain more consistent and the levels do not need to be as specific.

NOTE: PP1, PP2, and PP3 are preprimer book levels.

Book Levels

Knowledge of expectations for each stage of the reading continuum allows us to become better observers of student reading behaviors. This enables educators to select suitable materials for the individual child. Developmental stages go hand in hand with book levels. We initially used Reading Recovery™ recommendations for many books and then comparatively placed additional books at the same level. For the purpose of instruction, we have grouped book levels to correspond with the developmental stages of reading (see Figure 2.1). These book levels can be coordinated with the more traditional basal series that many school districts use. Our program defines the stages as the following:

- Emergent: Book Levels 1 through 4
- Beginning: Book Levels 5 through 8

- Transitional: Book Levels 9 through 13
- Expanding: Book Levels 14 through 20

As children progress past Level 20, they acquire more strategies building on the techniques they have previously learned. They become more independent at solving problems they encounter while reading more difficult books.

An excellent source of information about leveling books can be found in Chapter 6 of *Bridges to Literacy* by DeFord, Lyons, and Pinnell (1991). Leveling books is based on many criteria including repetition of words and phrases, types of sentence patterns, and how much support the illustrations offer. To build your own leveled book collection, begin by selecting a few books at each level from a variety of publishers that offer levels for their texts. Many children's book publishers are now leveling beginning reading books in their catalogs according to Reading Recovery™ levels. Once you collect a sampling of books, listen to several students read them aloud to familiarize yourself with the characteristics of each level. To build your library, add books from other sources that you will level using the previously leveled books as a guide. After estimating a book level, you can determine the accuracy of a level after a few children have read it. Do not hesitate to change the level if your first estimation was incorrect as there is no exact methodology in determining book levels.

There are many factors that influence how successfully children interact with a book. A child's *prior knowledge,* vocabulary, or the size of the print are just a few examples of why one child will succeed while another child might have trouble. For children to succeed they must be given ample opportunities to read, supportive instruction from the teacher while reading, and a variety of books within their level.

Prior knowledge—Any information children have learned about a topic before reading.

Explaining Developmental Stages and Book Levels to Parents

At the workshops, facilitators help parents learn where their children fall within the reading continuum. For parents, this awareness of developmental stages allows them to put things in perspective. They develop more realistic expectations and realize that with proper guidance their child will successfully progress, using a variety of strategies. Parents need to understand the relationship between book levels and developmental stages. Children can only learn to use a variety of strategies independently if the materials they are reading are at an appropriate level. Text is appropriate when it is easy enough for children to read fluently yet challenging enough for them to tackle new words and ideas. If too many words are unknown, children are unable to make sense of what they are reading and cannot self-monitor.

With a knowledge of the reading continuum and book levels, parents can develop better insight into which activities are more suitable at each stage. This makes parent-child reading time more rewarding and relaxing. All children benefit from working with supportive parents. This is especially true for children who are struggling and become frustrated when learning to read. Providing parents with the right amount of information and support through the workshops helps the home environment become more positive.

When books are sent home from our programs, they are easily recognized as they have a small round sticker in the upper-right-hand corner with the book level clearly marked. However, when parents and children self-select books, we teach them to identify appropriate materials using the following techniques:

- For Book Levels 1 through 4, parents should choose the books until their children become more capable readers. They can select a few appropriately leveled books and then allow their children to pick the books they want to read.

- For Book Levels 5 through 12, parents and children should use the 1-in-10 rule. If the reader makes more than 1 error in every 10 words they read, then the book is too difficult for the child to be reading.

- As children read books beyond Level 12, they can apply the five-finger rule when selecting books. Children randomly select a page in the book and attempt to read it. If they make more than five errors, the book is probably too difficult.

Parents and children alike begin to be able to compare books and know what is appropriate for them. If children are excited about reading a more difficult book, the book can be used for an adult to read aloud.

Jessica's Story

We will take you through the developmental stages using Jessica as an example of a typical reader in our support program. We will correlate the acquisition of reading strategies with the succession of book levels. Appropriate expectations will be provided at each level of reading for both the educator and parent to understand.

Jessica is a child who was exhibiting difficulty in learning to read in her regular classroom program. Her classroom teacher recommended she be given a reading assessment by the support teacher. It was determined that she knew the names of some letters and could supply sounds for several consonants. Jessica had a few *sight words* memorized. She took wild guesses at unknown words, using no strategies when trying to read independently. She exhibited some knowledge of one-to-one correspondence between speech and the written word. The support teacher determined that Jessica was reading at the emergent book level.

Sight words—Words that children identify immediately.

Emergent: Book Levels 1 Through 4

Before beginning to read, the teacher introduces the book by activating Jessica's prior knowledge through a *picture walk* and discussion. Books at this level have no more than a few sentences on a page. The text is highly repetitive with clear illustrations that support the text. First, Jessica and her teacher look at the cover and Jessica predicts what the book will be about. The teacher and Jessica then look at each page. Jessica describes what Halloween symbols she sees, and the teacher draws her attention to pictures that could help her with vocabulary as she reads. This is an authentic way of preteaching vocabulary that will be encountered in the story. It is more valuable than teaching words in isolation and supports using pictures as a strategy. The following is an excerpt from a reading lesson:

Picture walk—Looking at the pictures in a book before reading to help activate prior knowledge and vocabulary.

Teacher: We are going to read a book. Look at the cover. What do you think this book might be about?

Jessica: Halloween!

Teacher: Great prediction, Jessica. What do you think we might see on Halloween?

Jessica: Pumpkins, ghosts, black cats, witches, and candy.

Teacher: Good! You named a lot of things we see on Halloween. Let's look at the pictures. Maybe we will see some of your ideas and others in the book.

During the picture walk, the teacher will talk aloud about what she is thinking as she looks at the pictures. The teacher will ask Jessica to help predict what the story will be about. The teacher, by thinking aloud, models good predicting and shows how *prediction*s are based on information known at that time. The technique of thinking aloud demonstrates for learners how readers think as they read, and this can be used to model other strategy use.

Because Jessica has limited independent reading experience and few strategies, the teacher reads the story first, as she guides Jessica's hand pointing to each word. The reason for this is the teacher can model fluency, left-to-right progression, and one-to-one correspondence. The teacher will continue to guide Jessica's hand through other books until she is able to point to each word independently.

Prediction—What the reader thinks will happen in the story, based on the title, cover, pictures, and prior knowledge.

At the workshops, parents are taught that in any one stage, support may need to be modified as children progress. An adult prereading the story and children finger pointing will eventually not be necessary as children gain control over their reading. Once children acquire a bank of sight words, it is appropriate for readers to attempt the initial reading by themselves with adult support. We explain the importance of pointing until the child can sweep the page with their eyes without losing their place. Later, pointing becomes a technique some children use when they are experiencing difficulty with a phrase or a sentence.

The following dialogue continues after Jessica has heard the story read by her teacher and is now attempting to read it independently.

Jessica: Halloween (turns page)

Jessica: (pauses, then looks at pumpkin picture) The pumpkin

Teacher: Good Jessica, I like the way you used the picture to figure out the word *pumpkin*. Let's continue reading.

Jessica: The lady

Teacher: That was a good try, Jessica, because the picture shows a lady. Let's go back and look at the first letter of the word. Can this word be lady?

Jessica: It's a *w* so it can't be lady.

Teacher: Good Jessica, what sound does *w* make?

Jessica: /w/

Teacher: Great /w/ sound. Now look at the picture again. The person is wearing a costume and has a broom. Do you know what she is called?

Jessica: Oh, now I see, she's a witch. . . . The witch!

In this Halloween story, the teacher focuses on the repeated word *the* to be added to Jessica's sight-word vocabulary. She will help Jessica learn and remember it. For reinforcement, the teacher will help Jessica find the word *the* in other books they will read. The teacher can also add *the* to a word wall or create flashcards for practice.

Besides developing a sight vocabulary, Jessica is also beginning to learn to use strategies for figuring out unknown words. The teacher is reminding her to use picture clues as well as to look at the first consonant of the word to confirm the accuracy of her reading. Notice the teacher gives specific positive praise to Jessica that encourages continued use of the reading strategies.

As Jessica progresses, the teacher advances her to the next level. This is based both on the increased number of words recognized instantly and the ability to use the appropriate strategies at this level. The list of expectations is a general guide. Some children will require more time in mastering all the components of the emergent level.

Expectations for the Emergent Reader: Book Levels 1 Through 4

- Children understand that reading must be meaningful and tell a story.
- Children are able to follow the text with their finger left to right across the page. There is a one-to-one match, each word representing a spoken word.
- Children focus on beginning consonant sounds to figure out words.
- Children use pictures as one strategy to help them figure out a word.
- Children accumulate a bank of words recognized instantly. As reading levels increase, so does the number of words recognized automatically.
- Children may reread with more expression and *fluency.* (This goal never changes throughout the levels. Children may slow down to attempt a difficult word, but fluency resumes as soon as possible.)
- Children use pictures and text to predict what will happen in the story.

Fluency—The ability to read so it sounds like talking.

Parents should be reading aloud higher-level books to their children, modeling expressive reading. This is a good time for parents to be sharing a wealth of alphabet books with their children to reinforce beginning sounds. Parents can reinforce these sounds as their children are reading to them reinforcing at the same time other expectations on the emergent level.

Beginning: Book Levels 5 Through 8

At the beginning stage, new skills are introduced and developed while reinforcing previously learned strategies. Jessica is reading a book about a dog named Lois who is trained for use by visually impaired people. The book has about three sentences on each page. As in the previous lesson, Jessica and the teacher take a picture walk. Jessica is now ready to begin the initial reading without an adult prereading the book. The teacher asks Jessica to predict the story by looking at the cover and going through the pictures. Jessica's teacher reminds her that she should think about her prediction while reading. As Jessica begins to read, she makes a typical error one might see at this level. Her teacher prompts her to use strategies she has been taught.

Jessica: Lois went after the cat.

Teacher: Good Jessica! You can tell from the picture that Lois went after the cat. Look at this word (points to ran). Can it be *went?*

Jessica:	No, it starts with an *r*.
Teacher:	Good, now cover the *r* with your finger. See the *a* and the *n*? That is a *chunk* you know. Can you remember what it is?
Jessica:	The /an/ chunk
Teacher:	Great! If this part of the word is /an/ and the beginning is *r*, what word could it be?
Jessica:	an . . . ran
Teacher:	Excellent Jessica, I like how you used the chunk to help you figure out the word. Now what can you do to make sure the whole sentence makes sense?
Jessica:	I can read the sentence again.

Chunk—A vowel and letters that follow in a single syllable.

At this level, the teacher actively guides Jessica toward the clues she needs to help her read. Instruction is focused on her looking through the word as a source of information to figure out unknown words. When Jessica corrects a word-recognition error, she needs to learn to reread the sentence to confirm that her new word choice makes sense. Jessica probably has not yet internalized every strategy taught to this point so that she could use them independently. The teacher reviews Jessica's prediction with her after the story and they discuss what aspects were like the author's and how the pictures and text helped with the predictions.

Expectations for the Beginning Reader: Book Levels 5 Through 8

- Children use strategies from previous book levels.
- Children can determine if a pair of words rhyme.
- Children check their prediction at the end of the story to see if it makes sense.
- Children demonstrate an awareness of endmarks when reading orally.
- Children reread from the beginning of the sentence to determine an unknown word or to check comprehension.
- Children begin to read to the end of the sentence using meaning to help figure out an unknown word.
- Children check the beginning and ending consonant of a word while reading.
- Children identify known chunks in a word.

At the workshops, we teach parents of children at this stage to reinforce these strategies at home. Parents can share rhyming stories or poems with their children to help develop an auditory awareness of rhyming chunks.

Parents can encourage their children to reread the text if the meaning or word does not make sense. In addition, when children are reading at home, parents can focus the children's attention on the endmarks to aid in expressive oral reading.

Transitional: Book Levels 9 Through 13

Jessica has learned to implement some strategies and is now reading books at the transitional stage. Although the teacher is still providing *prompts*, she expects Jessica to do the reading with less support and allows sufficient *wait time* for her to attempt self-correction. The books at these levels have more text on each page, and the pictures are becoming less supportive. Jessica should have a bank of sight words sufficient enough to recognize most of the text. The rest of the words are figured out by applying the strategies she has learned.

> **Prompt—**A specific hint given by the listener to help the reader use a strategy.

Now Jessica is reading a book about beavers building a dam. It has about five sentences on each page. As in the past, Jessica takes a picture walk and makes some predictions about the story. She begins the story and experiences some difficulty with the first sentence as illustrated in the following:

> **Wait time—**Time given to the reader before the listener offers help.

Jessica: Once there was a little beaver who was eating a. . .

Teacher: (after waiting) Let's remember that we don't stop but continue to read to the end of the sentence. (Jessica finishes the sentence without reading the unknown word.)

Teacher: I like the way you skipped the word and read to the end of the sentence. Why don't we go back and see if you can figure it out by finding parts of the word you may know?

Jessica: (frames the word with her fingers) Well, I know *t* and *w* say /tw/ and the word ends with g. But I don't know the middle sound.

Teacher: Great Jessica! Reread the sentence with the sounds you hear for that word.

Jessica: Once there was a little beaver who was eating a /tw/ . . . /g/ under a tree. Oh, twig! Once there was a little beaver who was eating a twig under a tree.

Teacher: Super, Jessica! I like the way you stretched out the word. You used a good reading strategy when you read to the end of the sentence.

Jessica finished the page and the teacher asked if her prediction made sense with what she had read so far. Periodically, while Jessica is reading, the teacher will stop and give her an opportunity to think about her reading. Jessica may want to adjust her prediction based on new information supplied by the author. This helps her maintain comprehension throughout the story, providing Jessica with time to use the think-aloud technique.

Expectations for the Transitional Reader: Book Levels 9 Through 13

- Children use strategies from previous book levels.
- Children begin to stop periodically to think about the story and summarize important events.
- Children identify and begin to apply known blends and consonant digraphs in unknown words.
- Children can take a rhyming chunk and apply it to an unknown word.
- Children begin to notice and apply word endings.
- Children look through the word from beginning to end to apply all known phonetic skills.

Parents continue to monitor fluency as children increase levels. When children reread, it should sound like talking with expression. If children are not fluent, it is harder to maintain story meaning. Some children have an easier time with fluency than others because they have better word recognition and an ability to decode more rapidly.

At this stage, we are looking to expand sight vocabulary and phonics knowledge to increase fluency. Parents can support this by using commercial or teacher-made word games.

Expanding: Book Levels 14 Through 20

Jessica has entered a more advanced stage of learning to read. The text is longer, the stories are more involved, and Jessica is trying to integrate all the strategies she has learned. By this time, the teacher expects Jessica to be more independent.

Inferences—Logical conclusions readers make based on what they have read.

Now Jessica is reading a beginning chapter book about a boy who is caught unexpectedly in a storm. This story is a good example because it not only requires Jessica to read it successfully but also involves some prior knowledge of the dangers associated with weather. She will use this knowledge to make *inferences* to help in understanding the author's message. Jessica's teacher may require her to reread a portion of the book at home. At this level, some children are assigned unread text to read at home with their parents as they may not be able to finish it in school. As the text gets longer, the story should not be read completely aloud as the children are encouraged to practice some silent reading.

Jessica is reading a page to her teacher. Notice how independent she has become since the emergent level.

Jessica: As the sky darkened, Marco grab his little sister's hand and being to run for shelter. No wait not grab, grabbed . . . Marco grabbed his little sister's hand and being to run for shelter.

Teacher: (waits until Jessica reads to the end of the page) I really like how you went back and fixed *grabbed* by yourself. Can you reread this sentence? Something didn't sound right to me (teacher points).

Jessica: (rereading the sentence) It's *being* that's the wrong word (frames word with her fingers). I see *be* in the word. . . . Hmm.

Teacher: (after waiting for Jessica to try several strategies) You found the right word and got the beginning sound correct. What else can you do to help yourself?

Jessica: I see the /an/ chunk . . . an . . . gan . . . began oh, now I get it. As the sky darkened, Marco grabbed his little sister's hand and began to run for shelter. Oh I understand, the sky is getting dark so they are running for shelter before it rains.

Teacher: Good, Jessica! I like how you found a chunk and fixed the sentence. You are also right about the weather, darkening clouds usually mean rain.

Jessica has taken over much of the monitoring of her own reading. As children approach Book Level 20, they are reading silently more often and should be self-monitoring when they make a mistake. Parents should continue to periodically monitor their children's strategy use by listening to them read a few pages. Children may remain in this stage for some time. They are integrating all they have learned in longer, more complex text. They are required to do more thinking about what the author is saying. This should be expected, and parents need to understand that their children are learning a lot of information about the process of reading.

Expectations for the Expanding Reader: Book Levels 14 Through 20

- Children apply all previously learned reading strategies to check for meaning and self-correct what does not make sense.
- Children do not give up, but try every possible strategy they know before asking for help.
- Children adjust fluency depending on the difficulty of the material being read.
- Children concentrate on the author's message when discussing the story and use details to support conclusions.

- Children extend knowledge of vowel patterns in single-syllable and multisyllable words.
- Children begin to read easy chapter books silently.

At this stage, parents need to provide children with a wealth of literature representing a variety of genres. They should be encouraging their children to read silently more often, occasionally checking their reading aloud. Parents should place a greater emphasis on comprehension and story discussions.

Expectations for Readers Beyond Book Level 20

Once children surpass the expanding stage they are reading more independently. Our goal is to develop readers that are able to do the following:

- Read aloud with fluency and phrasing that assists comprehension.
- Read an increasing number of words automatically.
- Utilize decoding skills rapidly.
- Understand more difficult vocabulary.
- Monitor their own reading, checking that what they are reading makes sense.
- Read silently and independently.
- Extend their reading skills and strategies to a variety of genre, reading for many purposes.
- Make inferences about the underlying meaning of the text.
- Use the text as a source of information.

Although children are now reading more independently, parents still play an important role. Parents can read their children's text ahead of time to familiarize themselves with the material. This allows them to accurately monitor comprehension. This applies to both fiction and nonfiction content area textbooks.

Maintaining Home Contact

One of the highlights of this program is the continuous support that we offer parents and children. The take-home folder accompanies the children's book selections each time they are sent home. The folder contains a log

Figure 2.2. Sample Reading Log

Date Due	Reading Log	☆	Parents, please sign this after your child has read it to you at least once.
	☆		
	Parent's Comments		
	☆		
	Parent's Comments		
	☆		
	Parent's Comments		
	☆		
	Parent's Comments		
	☆		
	Parent's Comments		
	☆		
	Parent's Comments		
	☆		
	Parent's Comments		
	☆		
	Parent's Comments		
	☆		
	Parent's Comments		

where books are listed that have been sent home (see Figure 2.2). There is also a section where parents can communicate with the teacher. We suggest that parents write positive comments about their children's reading, which we share with the children when they return the folder. Parents use this opportunity to let us know how the reading session went and if they noted any strategy use. We help parents stay current by noting progress in their children's reading.

Educators must be practical about how much reading parents are able or willing to do at home with their child. You will find there is a wide range of abilities and interest among parents in supporting their struggling readers. It is most important that parents listen productively to their children's rereading and encourage appropriate strategy use. How much parents will do in addition to that is really an individual commitment. It is best to offer a variety of activities, but know that realistically only portions of it might be done by some parents and that is acceptable. Avoid being judgmental of parents' ambitions. Learn to accept any help that is given.

Teachers' and parents' awareness that reading is a developmental process is vital when supporting all readers, especially struggling ones. Both must understand that children will acquire a repertoire of strategies at their own pace with the outcome being children who can monitor their own reading. The appropriate use of book levels and a variety of genres will allow readers to successfully gain the knowledge and confidence they need to become independent readers. Our book levels and expectations are meant as a guide, keeping in mind the individual differences that are present among readers. The important aspect of the program is the continued growth and love of reading our children must experience.

Reference

DeFord, D. E., Lyons, C. A., & Pinnell, G. S. (1991). *Bridges to literacy.* Portsmouth, NH: Heinemann.

Using Phonics
Meaningfully

Numerous books have been written about the importance of phonics in reading instruction. It is important, though, to place this topic in perspective for parents so that it is not an overused strategy. When phonics is overemphasized and used as the single means of word attack, children learn to ignore meaning cues, and comprehension is adversely affected. Too often, children's reading is interrupted for meaning-less word errors because adults think that reading needs to be perfect. Nagy (1988), in summarizing research, reports that as many as 15% of the words in the text can be unknown and meaning can still be maintained. Through our program, parents learn that children's reading should seldom be inter-rupted, and readers need to be given the opportunity to self-correct their own errors using strategies appropriate to their reading level.

Phonics is only one of the strategies readers are taught to use to figure out unfamiliar words. For phonics to be a valuable strategy, children must be able to rely consistently on accurate sounds. Good readers use *decoding* skills rapidly to figure out unknown words, check the context to confirm the accuracy of their choices, and then return to fluent reading. Adams (1994) concurs noting, "Laboratory research indicates that the most critical factor beneath fluent word reading is the ability to recognize letters, spelling patterns, and whole words effortlessly, automatically and visually. The central goal of reading comprehension depends critically on this ability" (p. 54). When readers spend too much time figuring out new words, they often are unable to devote enough of their attention to story comprehension.

At our workshops, we provide parents with an overview of how we teach phonics and what they can do at home to support their children's learning. We teach them how to recognize when their children are developmentally ready for a particular aspect of phonics instruction. These aspects are crucial because parents need to understand how to integrate phonics supporting the use of alternate strategies when reading at home. This chapter discusses

Decoding—The ability to figure out unknown words using a variety of strategies.

27

the role phonics instruction and techniques play in children's total reading program.

Phonemic Awareness

Phonemic awareness— The understanding that a spoken word is made up of individual sounds.

Phonemic awareness is the understanding that a spoken word is made up of individual sounds. Children should be able to hear the sounds in words and learn to sequence those they hear. Phonics instruction builds on these prerequisite skills by showing how phonemes are represented in the printed word: "It is unlikely that children lacking phonemic awareness can benefit fully from phonics instruction since they do not understand what letters and spelling are supposed to represent" (Juel, Griffith, & Gough, 1986, p. 243). As children become cognizant that words are made up of phonemes or sounds, they realize that this can help them read and spell. They learn to manipulate letter sounds in words and syllables by taking words apart and blending sounds together. Research suggests that phonemic awareness may be the most important factor separating normal and disabled readers (Adams, 1994). Children who become good readers enter school with a well-developed sense of phonemic awareness. They have been read to frequently from a variety of books. These children have an awareness of rhymes in poetry and music, and they can identify many alphabet letters and the sounds they make. All of the literacy experiences they have had provides them with the tools they need to learn to read.

There are children who may still struggle with beginning reading and be unable to apply phonics, even though their parents have provided them with plenty of oral phonemic activities. They could have other weaknesses that affect their learning. These children may be unable to discriminate between sounds, have a poor memory, or have an inability to blend together sounds they hear. To strengthen these deficiencies, children should participate in phonemic awareness activities designed to encourage readiness for phonics while engaging in reading appropriately leveled books. Reading instruction does not have to wait until children know all their letters and sounds. Children having trouble with phonics can rely on other strategies as they begin to learn to read. They can build a sight-word vocabulary and use picture clues, adding phonetic strategies as they are able to apply them.

When children lacking phonemic awareness are enrolled in our reading programs additional support is provided. They engage in activities that combine oral language and phonics instruction. These activities include rhyming words, combining onsets and rimes, initial consonant substitution, identifying and changing medial vowel sounds, and listening for syllables. Children benefit from the support offered by integrating oral language and phonics skills together.

Sample Emergent Reading Lesson

Described below is a sample lesson for an emergent reader incorporating a phonemic awareness activity into a reading lesson focusing on beginning sounds. The teacher reviews the target letter sound with the group using the activity titled Initial Sound Switch (Blevins, 1998). The children are invited to play a word game where they will switch the beginning sound of a word. For example, say that /p/ is our target sound. When the teacher says the word *can*, one child would say the word *pan*. Play would continue with other words such as hat, shop, locket, Denny, and fond until each child has an opportunity to substitute the target letter and form a new word. The teacher would then read a book, chosen because the target letter appears frequently, aloud to the group. The students are then given an opportunity to read that book aloud.

After discussing the story, children can hunt for the target letter in the text, saying the words they find and highlighting the letter. The children are given the book to take home to reread with their parents and are instructed to bring in something from home that begins with the target letter sound.

Penny Push (Fitzpatrick, 1997) is another valuable phonemic awareness activity that encourages children to listen for sounds in words. Teachers should model this procedure several times. Each child is given a card with five or six horizontally drawn connected boxes on a 5 by 8 notecard. A penny or counter is placed under each box. As a word is said, the children push a penny or counter in the box for each phoneme heard. For example, children are pushing three pennies for the word f-u-n and f-i-sh. The word s-t-a-m-p has five phonemes. You can use pictures to prompt a word or use a word from the story. As the children encounter success at three and four pennies, increase the task to include five or six phonemes.

Parental Support for the Emergent Reader

Parents can help develop their children's phonemic awareness by reading aloud to them. We suggest that parents read poems and stories filled with rhymes and alliteration emphasizing the sounds. Parents and children can recite nursery rhymes together and share a wealth of alphabet books. Many authors such as Dr. Seuss and P. D. Eastman use rhyme effectively, and their books are particularly appealing to young children. Children learning to read love to experiment with language. They use riddles, silly songs, tongue twisters, and word games to manipulate sounds. Some of the familiar classic games, such as "We Are Going to The Beach" can be played while riding in the car. The first person starts off with saying, "I am going to the beach and I am bringing an apple." The next person continues the game with, "I am going to the beach and I am bringing an apple and a blanket," and so forth, seeing how far they can get through the alphabet. For younger children, parents may need to remind them of the letter that comes next.

Another popular game frequently played in the car, restaurants, and so on is Chategories. After a category has been chosen, such as people's names, states, foods, toys, and so forth, the first person names an item. For instance, if the category is *foods*, the first person could say "bread." The next player would have to name a food that starts with the last sound, /d/, such as doughnut. Play continues until you finish or change categories. These are ideal activities to foster the use of beginning and ending letter sounds. An excellent resource for other activities is Fitzpatrick's (1997) book, *Phonemic Awareness: Playing With Sounds to Strengthen Beginning Reading Skills.* It offers many useful oral and written phonemic activities. Other game book titles are available at the end of the chapter.

These activities develop children's auditory abilities, which prepare them for more formal instruction in phonics. To link phonemic awareness to beginning phonics, parents can create simple alphabet books with their children. They can use magazines or computer graphics to find pictures that correspond with a particular letter sound. These books become a letter sound dictionary and can be used as a reference when children forget a sound while spelling.

Introducing Onsets and Rimes

Onset—The initial consonant sound or consonant blend.

As children progress in reading, we teach them how to use beginning consonants, blends, and consonant digraphs as aids to figuring out unfamiliar words. When students can move beyond looking at just initial consonant sounds, they are ready to look for patterns in words by using onsets and rimes. *Onsets* are the initial consonant sound or consonant blend. The *rime* is the vowel and the letters that follow in a single syllable. Separating onsets and rimes is easier than fully segmenting a word and trying to sound out each individual letter. For example, you could segment the word *scratch* into /scr/ and /atch/. If you divided each sound individually, a child would need to blend seven sounds to get the word *scratch*, and most children would have difficulty blending that many sounds. When breaking up words, we teach children to look for the largest possible chunk they recognize.

Rime—The vowel and the letters that follow in a single syllable.

Children learn to look for patterns in words and syllables and use these rimes to build other words. Struggling readers must be exposed to a great deal of reading to acquire a bank of rimes. They are taught to look at the structure of words when reading, and teachers need to spend time helping children decode these words.

We introduce rimes in the following sequential order and have children look for these chunks when reading:

- Short-vowel rimes; examples include: at, in, ig, ip, on, up
- Long-vowel rimes; examples include: oan, eap, ine, ule
- R-controlled rimes; examples include: ord, ort, art, irt
- Variant-vowel rimes; examples include: ow, oil

There are 38 common rimes that with beginning blends, can account for 654 different one-syllable words. These same rimes can be found in many multisyllabic words (Fry, 1998). Children's knowledge of these rimes greatly increases their phonetic abilities. They are listed below in rank order based on frequency.

-ay, -ill, -ip, -at, -am, -ag, -ack, -ank, -ick, -ell, -ot, -ing, -ap, -unk, -ail, -ain, -eed, -y, -out, -ug, -op, -in, -an, -est, -ink, -ow, -ew, -ore, -ed, -ab, -ob, -ock, -ake, -ine, -ight, -im, -uck, -um

Sample Activities for Practicing Phonics

Games and activities can be sent home for parents to use as a reinforcement tool. We have explained a few that we share with parents. These techniques can be shared with parents at the workshops, at Back to School Night, or sent home with written explanations as assignments. The concepts are introduced in the context of reading, and they are then practiced in a format that reduces the use of other strategies, forcing children to look more closely at the spelling of the word and applying the phonetic generalizations.

After introducing the concept of onsets and rimes, Words in a Bag is a good follow-up activity (Kaye, 1984). This activity allows children to practice blending together parts of words. Children can work together in pairs, attempting to identify if what they have created is a word. The activity is prepared as follows:

1. Two brown paper bags for each team.
2. Two packages of 3-by-5 index cards; one white and one any color.
3. A list of 20 onsets and rimes. (We recommend using Fry's [1998] list as a beginning.)
4. Cut all index cards vertically in half.
5. Take 10 white index cards and record a rime on each one.
6. Take 10 colored index cards and record the onsets.
7. Place all the rimes into one bag and the onsets into the other bag.

To play the activity, use the following steps:

1. Give one set of premade cards to each parent/child team.
2. The child selects a card from each bag.
3. The child places the colored card in front of him or her first and the white card after it.
4. The child player attempts to read the combination.
5. The child records his or her combination on paper and circles all of those that are really words.
6. The next player takes a turn.
7. Play continues until all cards have been used.

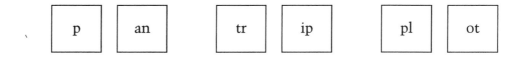

Making words with magnetic letters is another activity used in school. We purchase plastic letter sets where the consonants are one color and the vowels are in a contrasting color. This offers a visual aid to children when learning about onsets and rimes. We place the letters in alphabetical order on a metal surface such as a cookie tray. Children are taught to make patterns with the letters using them for consonant substitution in words. For example, if children form the word /camp/, they are asked to make other rhyming words such as stamp, tramp, champ, and cramp. Children at this point are simply changing the initial consonant sounds. As children develop this skill, they are expected to spell the entire word independently from dictation. This serves the dual purpose of reinforcing initial consonant sounds as well as the vowel rime. The teacher relates the activity to reading, in which children are taught to place their fingers like a frame surrounding the known chunk in an unfamiliar word. By reading the chunk they are then able to figure out the word.

Sound boxes are another hands-on technique that is excellent for extending phonics applications beyond using the initial sound. Some struggling readers attend only to beginning or ending sounds and need further instruction hearing the whole word. Sound boxes focus children's attention on the sequence of the sound-symbol relationships in the whole word. We have found this technique requires little teacher preparation so it becomes a practical tool for students to eventually use in proofreading by themselves for more accurate spelling. This technique should be incorporated into a reading lesson so that the words are introduced in meaningful context. It can be used prior to reading to familiarize students with a few new words, or at the end of the lesson for dealing with the words that gave children trouble.

As with any new activity, the teacher should model the procedure first so children clearly understand the directions. The word is said, stretching it out slowly and naturally. The children and teacher decide how many sounds they hear, and they then draw a box for each sound. Then the children place the sounds they heard in each box. When the children first use this procedure, they may be unable to hear the sounds in sequence. Some children will also have difficulty hearing all of the sounds and may need to be prompted to add other sounds. Accept what they can do and their abilities will increase once they become more familiar with the procedure.

When choosing words for sound boxes, initially there should be an exact match for each sound and symbol, such as s-t-o-p. As children's phonics knowledge increases, so can the words they attempt to spell. For example, b-oa-t, thr-i-ll, or shr-i-m-p can be tried.

Teachers also use word sorts, which are mind-stretching activities that allow children to search for sound and spelling patterns, which encourages them to analyze words in an enjoyable way (Henderson, 1990). Children are given a list of words, each on a separate index card. They then sort the words into different piles depending on some feature the words share. To model the activity, the teacher decides on the criteria for the sort using rhyming or vowel patterns, initial or ending sounds, or number of syllables. As children gain experience with the activity, they can decide how the words are grouped with the teacher checking their results. When they select the criteria for sorting independently, they are searching through the words to find similarities that link the words together. As children progress, the number and difficulty of the word cards can be increased.

Multisyllabic Words

As readers encounter more challenging text, there will probably be a greater number of *multisyllabic* words that will be unfamiliar to them. Good readers seem to be able to identify syllables, recalling recognizable riming chunks they have learned in one-syllable words and applying them to these new, longer words. For those children who do not find it so automatic, direct instruction may be needed. Understanding syllables aids in reading and spelling longer words.

When trying to spell multisyllabic words, children should first determine how many syllables they are encountering. They are taught to apply known sounds to each syllable just as they did with one-syllable words. They are then able to break down a word such as *category* into four manageable parts decoding it without assistance.

There are several ways to show children how to count syllables. Children can be taught to place a hand, palm-side down, underneath their chin when saying the multisyllabic word. Each time their chin touches their hand they

Multisyllabic—A word with more than one vowel sound.

know that a syllable has been spoken. Children are often told to clap syllables or tap a different finger on their desk each time a syllable is heard.

Teachers explain contractions, prefixes, suffixes, and compound words. Children can be taught to use prefixes and suffixes to help decode longer words. Affixes can be used to provide meaning clues as well as supply pronounceable chunks (Cunningham, 1995).

Vocabulary building during guided reading and content area lessons also helps to strengthen word knowledge. Encouraging children to use these new, longer words in their own writing is also important.

Sample Activity for Multisyllabic Words

After introducing the concept of multisyllabic words, teachers can play a game that reinforces this skill. Teachers create multisyllabic word cards that are placed in a stack on any blank gameboard. Each player in turn draws a card and reads the word aloud, identifying the number of syllables in the word. If the player guesses correctly they move their game piece. Instead of using dice, the piece is moved the same number of spaces as identified syllables.

In closing, parents should be aware that phonics is just one strategy in reading and not an end in itself. Phonics is best introduced in a meaningful context so that children see the need for the skill. Comprehension should never be sacrificed for phonics. Parents must be aware that every child will not be equally adept at auditorily identifying all the sounds and may only be able to use some of the phonetic elements.

References

Adams, M. J. (1994). *Beginning to read: Thinking and learning about print.* Cambridge, MA: MIT Press.

Blevins, W. (1998). *Phonics from A to Z: A practical guide.* New York: Scholastic.

Cunningham, P. (1995). *Phonics they use: Words for reading and writing* (2nd ed.). New York: HarperCollins.

Fitzpatrick, J. (1997). *Phonemic awareness: Playing with sounds to strengthen beginning reading skills.* Cypress, CA: Creative Teaching Press.

Fry, E. (1998). *Phonics patterns: Onsets and rime word lists.* Laguna Beach, CA: Laguna Beach Educational Books.

Henderson, E. (1990). *Teaching spelling.* Boston: Houghton Mifflin.

Juel, C., Griffith, G., & Gough, P. (1986). Acquisition of literacy: A longitudinal study of children in first and second grade. *Journal of Educational Psychology, 78,* 243-255.

Kaye, P. (1984). *Games for reading.* New York: Pantheon.

Nagy, W. E. (1988). *Teaching vocabulary to improve reading comprehension.* Newark, DE, & Urbana, IL: International Reading Association and the National Council of Teachers of English.

Additional Sources for Games and Activities

Cunningham, P., & Allington, R. (1999). *Classrooms that work: They can all read and write.* New York: Addison-Wesley.

Cunningham, P., & Hall, D. (1994). *Making big words: Multilevel, hands-on spelling and phonics activities.* Torrance, CA: Good Apple.

Cunningham, P., & Hall, D. (1994). *Making words: Multilevel, hands-on, developmentally appropriate spelling and phonics activities.* Torrance, CA: Good Apple.

Cunningham, P., & Hall, D. (1997). *Making more words: Multilevel, hands-on phonics and spelling activities.* Torrance, CA: Good Apple.

Ekwall, E., & Shanker, J. (1992). *Locating and correcting reading difficulties.* Englewood Cliffs, NJ: Prentice Hall.

Kaye, P. (1995). *Games for writing.* New York: Pantheon.

Lieberman, L. (1995). *FolderGames for phonics plus.* Palo Alto, CA: Monday Morning Books.

Love, M. (1983). *20 decoding games.* Torrance, CA: Fearon Teacher Aids.

Rockwell, R., Hoge, D. R., & Searcy, B. (1999). *Linking language: Simple language and literacy activities throughout the curriculum.* Beltsville, MD: Gryphon House.

Responding
to Literature

Although parents listening to their children reread books is instrumental in promoting fluency and word recognition, it is the conversations about texts that invite children to participate in the reading process. Sharing ideas about stories engages children's imaginations and develops a love of reading. Ideally, literacy development begins way before children enter school when parents read aloud to them. It continues as children enter school and take on the responsibility for reading themselves. If a child begins school without this important prerequisite to reading, schools must be prepared to provide additional reading support. All children, regardless of reading ability, should be expected to get meaning from print and be encouraged to share their thinking in discussions about what they have read: "Challenged learners who engage regularly in rigorous conversations about texts begin to anticipate engagement in meaningful dialogue and engage in more-intensive monitoring of their own comprehension" (Hoyt, 1999, p. 2).

With appropriate instruction, most children successfully engage in the literacy activities of reading, writing, speaking, and listening as they proceed easily through the developmental continuum. Yet, there are other children who encounter varying difficulties in obtaining meaning from text. The workshops extend parental knowledge and involvement by demonstrating how to support their children's story comprehension through oral discussion and written work.

We discuss the following questions in this chapter:

- How do we guide children, in school, who demonstrate weak comprehension skills to an increased understanding?

- What do we need parents to understand so they can encourage their children to respond meaningfully to literature in both discussion and writing?

- How do we enlist parental support in extending comprehension without it being overwhelming?

As educators, we no longer think of comprehension instruction as an exposure to a series of activities based on discrete comprehension skills: "Research does not support the identification of any set of comprehension skills, nor is there specific evidence that teaching students main-idea, sequence, cause-and-effect or other skills will make them better comprehenders" (Cooper, 1993, p. 6). We teach comprehension from a holistic viewpoint and not with an isolated skill-driven curriculum. Teachers instruct students to use certain behaviors before, during, and after reading that foster thinking about the text. Predicting, using prior knowledge, summarizing, inferencing, visualizing, self-questioning, and rereading if something does not make sense are a sampling of strategies readers are expected to use.

Parents are taught to observe their children's reading behaviors, making judgments as to when to offer support. Initially, the adult, using questions, directs the students' thinking. As children's literacy abilities develop, the responsibility for monitoring thinking moves from the adults to the children themselves. The type of prompts that parents offer will change, helping the children to become more independent and responsible for their own learning. Just as adults use prompts in helping children figure out unfamiliar words, there are meaning prompts to encourage thinking during reading. The prompts may start with "Look at the beginning sound. What word would make sense here?" and move to "What strategy can you use to help yourself make sense of that sentence?" Prompts are used as needed by parents when listening to their children read and in conversations they have with their children about text, as well as when they are writing together.

Discussing Stories Aloud

When parents are reading or listening to their children read aloud, it is imperative that they generate conversations about the story. The listeners should not assume just because children read fluently they are getting meaning from the text. Discussions should take place before, during, and after the actual reading. This allows children to prepare for reading, reflect on the text, and better comprehend. Although we use many techniques at school to develop self-monitoring, when teaching parents at the workshops we focus on making predictions, retelling stories, and asking key questions. This provides them with a basic guide to use at home without the task becoming overwhelming.

Making Predictions

As Adams (1998) suggests, "The process of comprehending involves not just understanding what one has read, but anticipating what one will read" (p. 99). Children are taught to predict the content of a story from the moment they see its cover illustration and the title. This strategy can be extended by taking a picture walk of the book at the earlier levels when illustrations support text. Predictions are an effective way to create an expectation about the story for the reader. They activate children's prior knowledge of a topic and help them recall previous personal experiences related to the story.

As children continue to read, they need to learn to stop reading periodically to check or adjust their predictions. Children learn to change predictions throughout their reading, attending to new information given by the author. A good example of this occurs when reading mysteries. The reader may have theories as to who the suspect is, but this can change as new clues are added. Usually the author provides readers with hints along the way, allowing them to make judgments about solving the mystery.

We train parents to encourage children to predict and use this as a strategy to improve comprehension throughout the story. Parents can ask children to make predictions before and during reading, which places the responsibility of monitoring on the reader. They can select points in the story to stop reading and ask their children questions such as "Is this what you thought would happen?" or "What do you think the character will do next?" Parents need to be accepting of their children's predictions even if they differ from the outcome of the story. Children bring different experiences to their reading, and this affects their predictions. However, these predictions should be based on the information given in the story.

Verbal Retelling

Retell—Relating a story previsously experienced.

A technique teachers use for assessing comprehension that parents can adapt for children is to *retell* what has been read. This gives the listener insight into how the readers are relating to the text. Adults can listen to how well children summarize, infer, and identify important information. They can also note if their children are adding untrue details or leaving out important parts of the story. By retelling stories, from both text and actual life experiences, children become accountable and take responsibility for what they want to share. Hoyt (1999) confirms this by defining retelling as "a reflection tool that requires readers to organize information they've gleaned from the text in order to provide a personalized summary" (p. 39). The reader retells important events sequentially and relates the story to personal experiences. The summary can also include characters and their actions, problems and solutions, and settings.

Prompting a Retell

Sometimes children need prompting during a verbal retelling for a variety of reasons. It could be that readers are unsure of themselves or might not have the necessary language to convey their thoughts orally. They also might not have understood the authors message. Once in a while, children may not be familiar with the topic of the story or the specific vocabulary that was used. Even if children are retelling the story adequately, there are many that simply restate the factual details, not really reflecting on the meaning or relating the story to their own prior knowledge or experiences.

When prompting a retell, parents should aim for higher-level thinking skills. The questions need to go beyond just recalling facts into using the information to gain a deeper understanding of the author's message. Parents can ask about the setting and how it changes or affects the story. They might have their child identify the characters' problems, how the problems were solved, and other ways they might have been solved. The workshops provide parents with information on developing positive questioning techniques to promote higher-level thinking. These techniques can be found in the parent resource guide under the heading, Strategies Good Comprehenders Use. Holdaway (1994) suggests that the purpose of any reading program should be to produce the highest level of comprehension possible during actual silent reading. This can apply to parent-child reading as well, in preparation for silent reading. Parents are shown how the classroom program fosters thinking early in their children's reading instruction. The attempt is made to challenge readers to think and stimulate their interest in reading. When children are taught to support their inferences with details from the text, we know they are recalling enough factual information.

At the workshops, the facilitators demonstrate for parents how teachers use a *think aloud* technique in class. The teacher, while reading aloud, stops at predetermined points and verbalizes what she is thinking to help her make sense of the text and to figure out unknown words. This modeling shows the students how good readers monitor their own reading as they move through the story. At home, parents could model this when their children experience comprehension difficulties. They can read several pages of a book aloud while their child listens. Parents can stop and verbalize comments that demonstrate how they are using strategies to interact with the text, then encourage their children to participate in this activity.

Think aloud—Verbalization of one's thoughts during the reading process.

Facilitators at the workshops caution parents not to develop a questioning style similar to an interrogation. Parents can be helped to realize that after sharing text, there are generally only a few really important questions that need to be asked to show the children's understanding of the story. As with rereading, parents need to establish the same positive, supportive environment. Children need to feel comfortable in taking risks when participating in open dialogue. They will not be able to do that if the environment is tense.

Written Responses to Literature

Realistically, parents will engage in conversations about books more frequently than they will have their children respond in a written form. However, writing is a frequent tool of educators who wish to expand children's personal connection to the story. When written assignments come home from school, parents need to know how to help. We have found at the workshops that parents frequently ask what their role is in overseeing their children's writing. They often perseverate on the accuracy of their children's writing, not understanding that their children are producing developmentally appropriate work. Sometimes this causes writing to become a frustrating exercise that can discourage children's efforts. Once the parents are educated in the writing process, they are able to relax and are more capable of helping their children.

Getting Ready to Write

Just as they do in reading, parents should take an active role in their children's writing development from the onset. Parents should know what to expect from each writing stage. This information is provided in the parent resource guide.

Beginning writers' attempts to convey ideas about literature are often met with an inability to translate these ideas into a recognizable message. Often, children begin by scribbling, drawing pictures, or stringing letters together. We explain to parents that this is developmentally appropriate. Just as the emergent reader has a limited supply of strategies to use, children who are learning to write have limitations as well. They will eventually learn to translate ideas into written symbols that convey a message as they develop a sight-word vocabulary and gain better control over sound-symbol relationships. Parents can help by showing their children how speaking and writing go together. After reading a story aloud, parents can ask their child what he or she is thinking. They can say to the child, "I am going to write down what you say." The child can then watch the parent write down the message. Finally, the parent can read what was written.

Typically, as children show improvement in their reading, they start making strides in their writing. It is important for parents to understand both the reading/writing connection and the developmental nature of writing.

Beginning Writing

Once children demonstrate in their writing that they understand what a word is and have moved past stringing letters together, their responses to literature can be more easily read by others.

Primary teachers model writing processes, demonstrating the components of good writing. They think aloud, just as they did during the oral discussion, composing well-constructed sentences so the text is visible to all children. Early instruction typically revolves around getting ideas down on paper. The teacher also emphasizes initial consonants, spacing between words, and final punctuation. Children's abilities will determine the emphasis placed on the instruction. This modeling is interactive, with the children verbally giving input to the teacher while she is writing. The teacher solicits help from the children in order to engage them in the writing process. During the modeled lesson, children are not writing, but instead they are attending to the teacher-directed instruction, visualizing in their minds what good writers do when they are writing.

After teachers have modeled good writing, they may take small groups of children with similar writing skills for a guided writing lesson. The teacher and children both participate in the writing process. The teacher varies the amount of support depending on the needs of the children. We explain at the workshops that we expect more accuracy when writing is done with an adult as opposed to when children are working independently. This information helps parents understand that not all work needs to be done perfectly, and it also allows them to perceive the entire scope of the writing process.

At our workshops, we demonstrate how parents can work positively while writing to encourage their children's active participation. Parents of beginning writers need to establish a supportive environment. When parents and children are writing together at this beginning stage, we recommend certain techniques.

- The parent and child should be sitting side by side.

- The child should discuss with the parent what he or she wants to write.

- The child does the actual writing.

- As the child writes word by word, he or she works cooperatively to figure out the correct spelling.

- The child rereads the sentence as needed to maintain the meaning of what is being written.

- The parent provides specific praise and encouragement.

As children move toward independence in responding to literature, parental support shifts from close supervision to a more advisory capacity, requiring children to take greater risks. As children become more capable of handling reading that is lengthier and more complex, the writing is expected to keep pace.

Beyond Beginning Writing

As children progress through the stages of writing, the quality and quantity of their responses increase. Whereas in the earlier reading stages the writer was concerned with getting a more basic message across, now the effort goes toward conveying a deeper understanding of the text. They have expanded their vocabulary, which allows them to attend more closely to the meaning of what they are writing than to word recognition. The children increase their responses to higher-level inferencing questions when writing. The teacher will lead many open-ended discussions to encourage creativity and complexity in writing.

Samples of open-ended questions used to stimulate writing are listed below. The goal is to encourage children to use complex thinking about what they have read. You will notice that although these questions are teacher directed, they allow for a variety of responses from the children. They also require children to go beyond the text and pull in their own thoughts and ideas.

- What are the settings and how did they add to the story?
- How did the characters change during the story, and what contributed to their changes?
- What would you have done differently in the story to change the ending? Why?
- The characters faced many problems. How did they solve them, and what would you have done differently in their place?
- Retell the story from a different character's point of view.
- Compare the author's messages in several of his or her books.

Brainstorming—Listing ideas or alternative responses to a topic.

At home, parents may see these higher-level questions in content area assignments such as science and social studies. Some children experience difficulty with these types of questions, and parents may need to provide structure for the assignments. They may want to review the vocabulary or discuss the overall concepts that the author has conveyed. Parents can help by simply restating the question or *brainstorming* with their child possible responses. Children need to organize their thoughts aloud prior to writing. Parents can act as a sounding board, offering feedback to aid in the writing process.

When parents and children are writing together at this stage, we recommend certain techniques.

- The parent and child should concentrate on the deeper meaning of the text.
- Children should discuss what they are going to write.

- Children should make the initial attempt at answering the questions.

- Written responses should contain more complex language structures.

- In content areas, parents may need to assist with vocabulary and organization of ideas.

- Revising and editing are initially done by the child with parents helping when needed.

Revising and Editing

At the workshops, parents often express concerns regarding their children's inability to spell and edit correctly. The parents need to be made aware that spelling and grammar are components of the entire developmental framework of writing. For a while, parental concerns were fueled by the confusion surrounding whole language among educators and the media alike. Even parents in school districts that remained more traditional were unsure of how their children were being instructed in writing and how much support they needed to provide. This confusion led to parents providing too much or not the right type of support. As part of our program, we share with parents what their children may be required to do when preparing a final draft in school.

We suggest that children concentrate first on the content of their writing. They should make sure their answers are complete and address the question. Responses should be logical and in a sequential order. Checking the content's accuracy applies to all writing, not just answering questions.

Once children are satisfied with what they have written, they need to reread for grammar, punctuation, capitalization, and spelling errors. Even though children are expected to edit their own work, in the primary grades most children are not able to complete this task independently. The struggling writer will require more time and attention from an adult to acquire these skills. Our parents come to accept that their children will need more supervision when learning revising and editing skills. Over the years at our workshops, parents asked several questions on this topic.

How Accurate Does My Child's Spelling Have to Be?

Spelling is a developmental process that evolves over time. Beginning writers have a limited store of sight words they can spell accurately. They are instructed to use temporary spelling when needed. This allows children to write the sounds they hear and concentrate on their message. Parents are cautioned not to focus too heavily on exact spelling in a rough draft. This often limits beginning writers and creates children who will write only what they can spell correctly. Children need the opportunity to experiment with written language expression.

When children have previously spelled a word correctly, it is then expected that they will continue to spell that word correctly in subsequent writing. If the known word is misspelled, parents can prompt the child by asking, "Does this word look right?" The child should then make the correction with the parents help if needed. At this stage, initial and final consonant sounds should be represented in the words. If the child encounters difficulty with a particular sound, parents can help by slowly and clearly enunciating the word so the child can better hear individual sounds.

Writers who have passed the beginning stages and are on their way toward becoming conventional spellers should be able to recognize when a word does not look right and experiment with alternate spellings. Children should be evolving into responsible spellers who are accountable for their own corrections.

Why Doesn't the Teacher Correct
All of My Child's Writing Errors?

All teachers are individuals with different techniques and expectations for accuracy. Because writing is developmental, teachers generally do not expect beginning writers to be perfect when working independently. For example, during journal writing many teachers will be more flexible in allowing errors as long as the children have proofread their writing. The children's thoughts are the most important element and the teachers may encourage them to put their ideas down as best they can without worrying about errors in their writing.

As children progress through the grades, teachers raise their expectations for correct writing and parents may see more attention given to editing. This, of course, depends on the abilities of the individual child. Most important, the parent must remain in contact with the teacher to discuss the requirements for writing.

My Child Begins Sentences the Same Way.
How Can I Help Her to Vary Her Writing?

Beginning writers often keep their responses "safe" by using only the words they can correctly spell. This can lead to the same type of sentences being repeated on a daily basis. A child may write, "I like my dog" one day and "I like my cat" the next. The list of "I likes" may continue for weeks with no end in sight. Although this is part of the early developmental stages, children can become stuck in safe writing and lose some of their risk-taking abilities. Parents can begin by helping children to expand what they have already written. When a child writes "I like" repeatedly, the parent can ask questions to solicit more details about why the child likes that subject. The "I like my dog" sentence may become, "I like my dog because he licks my face."

The next step would be for parents and children to recall experiences they have shared and then write about them. This allows them to move away from the repetitious "I likes" to other topics. Brainstorming a list of ideas with children is a good way to help them overcome the problem of topic selection. The list can be in written form and they should keep it nearby to refer to when starting to write.

My Child Has Difficulty Initiating Writing. How Can I Help?

Brainstorming is a technique that also applies to this problem. Story starters are another idea that can help a child who has trouble getting started. This involves providing a beginning sentence that students build on to create a story.

For many writers, stating that they do not know what to write could actually be indicative of another problem. Teachers watch for other issues that might be the underlying cause of a child's inability to write. They could have visual or fine motor problems that make the task of writing extremely difficult. Some children may be perfectionists unwilling to write unless the size and shape of the letters meets with their approval. They spend an inordinate amount of time erasing perceived mistakes and overfocusing on correct spelling.

Children who have visual or fine motor problems may have many great ideas, but may have difficulty putting them down on paper. In this case, they should be allowed to dictate their stories into a tape recorder or to an adult. As time goes by, children can begin to combine writing with dictating and eventually take on most of the writing themselves. Classrooms or homes that are fortunate enough to have computers can allow children to learn keyboarding and type their stories.

Children who are perfectionists can make themselves so tense that writing becomes a chore. Parents and teachers can help by allowing themselves to make mistakes when writing. For instance, there are teachers who write a daily morning message on the board to their class that is intentionally full of spelling and grammar errors. The students are given a chance to help the teacher fix the message. Children often believe that adults are perfect; by simply allowing them to see otherwise, they will learn that mistakes are not the end of the world.

Parents are encouraged to provide their children with as many authentic opportunities as possible to write, beyond retelling stories from books. Letters to grandparents or friends who might have moved, shopping lists, keeping a journal, and a chore list are some ideas. Parents can discuss at the workshops ways they have successfully incorporated children's writing into their regular routines.

What Are Some Resources Children Can Use at Home When Editing Their Spelling?

When children reach a point where they are writing independently, there are several tools they can use to help them check their spelling. When children are through revising their written work, they check the content for spelling errors. Writers can review what they have written, underlining any words they think are incorrectly spelled. We suggest the use of colored pencils for this task as they stand out from the rest of the words. Once the misspelled word has been identified, children should attempt alternate spellings until they see one they believe is spelled right. They should incorporate phonetic rules when trying to fix the spelling. At this point, they can confirm the accuracy of the word with their personal dictionaries. A personal dictionary can be created out of a notebook in which children keep words they have previously had trouble spelling.

Parents should be encouraged to purchase dictionaries and thesauruses at an appropriate level. They should be readily available for use when writing.

How Can I Help My Child Spell Longer, Multisyllabic Words?

Children need to be able to hear syllables before being able to write them. Teachers show children several techniques for knowing how to count syllables. Children can put a hand just under their chin as they slowly say the word. A syllable is counted each time their chin touches their hand. They can also clap out syllables or put a finger down on the table each time they hear a syllable.

Once children identify how many syllables are in the word, we model how to work on the spelling of one syllable at a time. This allows them to hear all the sounds. The children are less nervous about using longer words and realize they have more control over the spelling rather than just guessing.

Students at all levels of instruction must be expected to read for meaning. Without meaning, they are simply reciting a list of words. Teachers model strategies including predicting, summarizing, inferencing, visualizing, and self-questioning in think-alouds. They demonstrate how these strategies can be used by readers to make sense of what they are reading. Teachers, then, attend to students' oral reading to assess how these strategies are being implemented. Teachers continue to monitor and prompt until the children are able to do it for themselves.

Parents can also be involved in this support system. They need to be made aware of the strategies as well as how to prompt with different levels of questions. The school program can be reinforced by showing parents how to engage their children in conversations about books, encouraging responses to open-ended questions. Students need to be challenged to answer questions, solve problems, or use information in new ways to attain higher-level thinking.

Children's writing can also be supported by parents while providing authentic uses for writing. Again, parents need to be aware of developmental milestones so they have appropriate expectations, especially concerning proofreading for accuracy.

Reading and writing are reciprocal in the literacy spectrum. When we enlist parental support in both avenues, we provide even greater opportunities for children to succeed as both readers and writers.

References

Adams, M. J. (1998). *Beginning to read: Thinking and learning about print.* Cambridge, MA: MIT Press.

Cooper, D. (1993). *Literacy: Helping children construct meaning.* Boston: Houghton Mifflin.

Holdaway, D. (1994). *Independence in reading.* Portsmouth, NH: Heinemann.

Hoyt, L. (1999). *Revisit, reflect, retell: Strategies for improving reading comprehension.* Portsmouth, NH: Heinemann.

Workshops 5

Now that we have provided you with a foundation to use, it is time to think about organizing and facilitating your own workshops. This chapter and the next explain the planning that is involved, what each workshop encompasses, and adaptations you may need to make.

Preparing for Workshops

After deciding what information we wanted to share with the parents, there were a few practical considerations we had to take into account before we began the actual workshops. We designed each workshop to be unique, with different purposes and separate agendas. Following is a list of questions we asked ourselves to prepare for the workshops.

Who Do We Invite to Each Workshop?

We find it most beneficial to have the first two workshops attended by parents only. We include parents of children enrolled in any of our school support programs. During these two workshops, we share a great deal of information with parents on how to positively work to support their children's reading and writing. They return home after each session and use the techniques we have discussed and modeled.

Parents and children are invited to our third and fourth workshops. We plan an agenda with the purpose of observing parent-child interactions. We watch for their ability to apply what has been learned in a real setting. This gives us a true indicator of how much skill has been attained and allows us to provide parents with positive feedback and ideas for improvement.

The inclusion of children in the workshops is truly exciting. We see positive interactions between parents and children sharing their love of

Figure 5.1. Sample Invitation to Workshop 1

Ms. Glass, Mrs. Peist, and Ms. Pike cordially invite the parents of their students to the first workshop.

THURSDAY, SEPTEMBER 23, 2000
7:00-8:30 PM
ELEMENTARY SCHOOL LIBRARY

Topics for discussion are the following:

1. Create a supportive reading environment
2. Discuss developmental nature of reading
3. Explain book levels
4. Learn to use appropriate prompts and praise
5. Parent question session

_____   Yes, I will attend the workshop.

_____   No, I am unable to attend this workshop.

Parent signature _____

Child's name _____

reading and writing. The students come filled with anticipation and ready to work. The enthusiasm they generate is contagious to everyone involved. Discussions at the beginning of the workshop are brief, explaining procedures and directions. Emphasis is on fast-paced hands-on activities.

How Can We Encourage Optimal Attendance?

We make a concerted effort to attract parents to attend our workshops. We send home flyers (see Figures 5.1 through 5.4), which include each evening's agenda. It is important that parents feel the topics are relevant and address their concerns. Because our Back to School night takes place in mid-September, we use that occasion to encourage parents to attend the first workshop in late September. A week before all workshops, we send home reminder notices and follow up with phone calls to the parents who do not respond to the flyers. It is important to encourage parents to attend the first

Figure 5.2. Sample Invitation to Workshop 2

Ms. Glass, Mrs. Peist, and Ms. Pike cordially invite the parents of their students to the second workshop.

WEDNESDAY, OCTOBER 27, 2000
7:00-8:30 PM
ELEMENTARY SCHOOL LIBRARY

Topics for discussion are:

1. Parent feedback: What's working? What's not?

2. Subgroups

Emergent and Beginning Readers

- Reading/writing connection

Transitional Readers and Beyond

- Reading/writing connection with realistic expectations for phonics and spelling in independent writing
- Supporting vocabulary development and comprehension

_____   Yes, I will attend the workshop.

_____   No, I am unable to attend this workshop.

Parent signature _____

Child's name _____

workshop because once they do, they are likely to return for subsequent workshops. The parents realize that unlike other large-group workshops, ours is more personal and directed to their specific needs.

When Should We Hold Our Workshops?

We schedule the first workshop as early as possible in the school year. Because we are sending home books for the children to reread, we want parents to be involved from the onset using the right techniques. The first time a book goes home in the reading homework folder, we accompany it with a letter explaining what the parents can do to help (see Figure 1.1). This letter is not meant as a substitute for parent training, but it is a way

Figure 5.3. Sample Invitation to Workshop 3

Ms. Glass, Mrs. Peist, and Ms. Pike cordially invite our students and their parents to the third workshop.

TUESDAY, FEBRUARY 22, 2001
7:00-8:30 PM
ELEMENTARY SCHOOL LIBRARY

Parents and children are invited to participate in the following three education stations:

A. Buddy reading

B. Reading games and activities

C. Interactive writing

Plus: Refreshments

_____ Yes, I will attend the workshop.

_____ No, I am unable to attend this workshop.

Parent signature _____

Child's name _____

to engage parents' help in a supportive manner, preparing them for the workshops. Usually our first workshop is held at the end of September and our second about a month later. This allows parents time to practice the techniques they have learned at home but still gives them an opportunity to seek help early in the year. The third and fourth workshops, which include children, are held in February and May.

Where Should We Hold the Workshops?

We are able to facilitate our workshops in our school library. This setting is an ideal place because it promotes a friendly, warm learning environment and is large enough without being overwhelming. We suggest that you try to find a spot in your school that evokes a similar feeling. If at all possible, stay away from large auditoriums that can make parents feel cut off from the presenters and each other.

Figure 5.4. Sample Invitation to Workshop 4

Ms. Glass, Mrs. Peist, and Ms. Pike cordially invite our students and their parents to the fourth workshop.

MONDAY, MAY 15, 2001
7:00-8:30 PM
ELEMENTARY SCHOOL LIBRARY

Celebration of reading success!
   Poems, skits, and shared reading

Getting ready for summer reading
   Reading tips and ideas

Presentation of certificates

Refreshments

Early responses are requested so that all children are able to participate in the evening's activities.

_____

_____   Yes, I will attend the workshop.

_____   No, I am unable to attend this workshop.

Parent signature _____

Child's name _____

How Should We Arrange the Room?

Once we have an estimate as to how many parents are attending, we alert our evening custodial staff of our intentions to hold the workshops. They will then arrange chairs ahead of time in three quarters of a circle formation. This configuration allows all parents to be facing the facilitators and each other. We want them to feel comfortable when addressing each other during open discussion times. At the entrance to the library we set up a desk with a sign-in notebook and name tags. The notebook allows us to keep an accurate attendance record. We also make sure to wear name tags ourselves so parents feel comfortable addressing us personally. Refreshments are in close proximity for easy access after the workshops.

What Equipment or Materials Will We Need?

We secure a television and VCR hookup for our first workshop to show our teacher-made video. Because the first two workshops involve parents being able to understand how to work with their children, we found that having a video to reinforce what was being learned is a big asset. After receiving parental permission, we videotaped three sample reading lessons at school. The lessons demonstrated techniques for supporting strategy use as well as exemplifying the positive interaction between teacher and student. We chose to show an emergent, beginning, and transitional reader so that our parents understand how children's strategies progress. After editing, each taped session lasted approximately 3 minutes.

In general, we keep a supply of pens and pencils for those parents who want to take notes in their parent resource guide. We also use a large write-on/wipe-off board. It serves as an easel to hang our charts (enlarged versions of our parent resource guide pages), and a place to write questions and concerns. You can easily substitute an overhead projector, which works just as well.

How Much Time Should We Allot for the Workshops?

We schedule our workshops from 7 PM to 8:30 PM. Starting at 7 PM allows the parents time after work to get the household in order before attending. Although we like to start on time, we allow a 5-minute cushion for parents who arrive late. During the workshops, we try to keep the informational or activity part to about an hour. Even though parents are invited to ask questions throughout, we leave time at the end for their clarifications. Finally, we offer refreshments, which provides parents with a time to talk to us individually about their concerns.

Agenda for Workshop 1

1. Distribute parent resource guide as parents arrive
2. Welcome, introductions, and statement of purpose of the workshops
3. Provide the following information from the parent resource guide:
   - Creating a supportive learning environment
   - Developmental reading ladder (supporting children's reading)
   - Selecting appropriate books
   - Being a good listener
   - Prompting the reader and using specific praise

4. Show demonstration video

5. Question-and-answer session

6. Distribute parent questionnaire

7. Have refreshments

As parents arrive, we distribute Part 1 of the parent resource guide, which allows them to peruse the information while waiting for the workshop to begin. A facilitator opens the workshop by introducing the presenters, stating the purpose of the workshops, and thanking the parents for attending. She also thanks those people who have supported the program, the principal, Board of Education, supervisors, and anyone who has provided funds and support.

When working with more than one facilitator, it is helpful to divide up the responsibilities for the presentation. Each facilitator can lead the discussion of a different topic so the evening is viewed as a collaboration. A comfort level is established, and the facilitators add informally to each others' presentations.

We proceed through the agenda directing parents' attention to the resource guide, teacher-made charts, and video. During our presentations, some parents like to take notes to clarify a point in order to make the parent resource guide meaningful to themselves. We authored the guide to be user-friendly, using educational jargon sparingly and defining those terms that we needed to include. Included at the end of this book is a reproducible parent resource guide.

During the question-and-answer period, facilitators work collaboratively, responding to questions in an open and straightforward manner. We then distribute questionnaires (see Figure 5.5) and ask parents to think about what they have learned and to return their reactions to us in a few days.

Agenda for Workshop 2

1. Welcome and brief recap of first meeting

2. Parents' feedback ("What's working? What's not?")

3. Provide the following information from second half of the parent resource guide:
   • Guiding comprehension
   • Sharing a story
   • The developmental writing stages

4. Divide the group into the following two groups:
   • Group 1—emergent and beginning reading and writing
   • Group 2—transitional reading and writing

Figure 5.5. Parent Questionnaire

Thank you for attending our first evening workshop. Your input and ideas are important to us. We ask that you take a few minutes to fill out the survey below and return it with your child as soon as possible. This will enable us to address any concerns at our next meeting. Feel free to write on the back of this paper if necessary.

1. How has your attendance at the workshop affected your working relationship with your child? _____

_____

2. Have you been successful at finding a quiet time and place to work with your child? Can you describe what works for you? _____

_____

3. What strategies have you noticed your child beginning to use independently? _____

_____

4. What information do you feel you still need to work successfully with your child? _____

_____

5. Do you have any questions or concerns that you would like to discuss at the next workshop? _____

_____

---

5. Create an open forum for parental problems and concerns

6. Have refreshments

We begin this workshop a half hour earlier for parents who were unable to attend the first workshop. We briefly provide them with needed information and distribute the parent resource guide from the first workshop. Because this is an abridged version of the previous workshop, we invite parents to call us if they have any concerns. We also integrate this information when we speak to parents at conference time in November.

After everyone has arrived, we work together with parents to create a two-column chart called "What's Working?/What's Not?" We open the discussion with parents and ask them to share their experiences, trying to create a comfortable environment using strategies and working with their children. Parents share their many successes about what they changed in the way they listened to their children read. When parents express concerns over what is not working, parents and facilitators brainstorm solutions and share what worked for them in similar situations.

After sharing, we divide into groups with one consisting of emergent and beginning readers and the other with the transitional readers. Prior to our second workshop, we color code parents' name tags based on their children's developmental level. This allows parents to find their place easily as we are separating them by developmental—not grade—level. In the emergent and beginning group, the facilitators discuss the relationship between reading and writing. They demonstrate how parents can work with children in an interactive writing experience. Techniques to support this concept will be experienced in Workshop 3 at one of the participation stations.

The second group discusses how to activate prior knowledge, predicting, story meaning, and the different types of comprehension questions that parents should ask when sharing a story with their children (see Chapter 4). We explain that techniques can be used either during parent read-alouds or when the child is the reader. We then talk about writing, helping parents create realistic expectations for spelling and phonics use. Using the writing stages from the resource guide, parents are made aware of what is appropriate at each stage and what to encourage in their children's writing.

Agenda for Workshop 3

1. Provide an overview of participation stations
2. Create the following three participation stations that every parent-child team will visit:
   - Station 1—book selection and buddy reading
   - Station 2—reading activities and games
   - Station 3—interactive writing response
3. Have refreshments

Prior to the meeting, we divided the parent-child pairs into three groups based on approximate developmental reading levels, not by grade level or teacher. We color-code name tags so that parent-child pairs can easily find their stations. Because all three stations are visited, the tags eliminate any confusion when it is time to change. We allot 20 minutes for each station and have a facilitator supervise each one. Although we have enough facilitator support to run these stations simultaneously, you may have to adapt the stations to meet your needs (see Chapter 6).

Station 1: Book Selection and Buddy Reading

Station 1 is divided into two parts. The first 5 minutes are devoted to explaining how to choose appropriate books to read. The facilitator notes that, when choosing a book from a library or bookstore, it is not always reliable to look at the reading level stated by the publisher. For example, a book that says it is for Grades 1 through 3 or ages 2 through 8 is too large a spectrum, making it meaningless for determining readability. Because there is little standardization between publishers when leveling books, parents are encouraged to use the techniques from the resource guide. An enlarged version of the five-finger rule page is displayed as a reminder.

The next 5 minutes focus on a review of the "A Good Listener Will . . ." chart taken from the resource guide. Then two facilitators role-play an appropriate and inappropriate buddy reading. If two facilitators are not available, you may plan with a reliable parent to act as a partner.

The last 10 minutes consist of children taking their parents to a collection of books and selecting one to read. The collection contains several shelves that have been set aside with leveled text. We make sure to remove the text number so the parent-child teams have to try the five-finger or 1-in-10 word rule to see if the book is appropriate. The parent and child discuss whether their book choice is successful.

The interaction between the parent and child is very interesting to observe. Facilitators are free to circulate and offer praise as to how well the teams are working together. Remember to keep the praise specific to encourage the correct strategies in the reader and listener.

"Mrs. P, that was wonderful how you gave your son extra time to figure out that word!"

"David, you did a good job by showing your dad how you used the beginning sound to figure out that word."

"Jodi, you and your mom are really working great together. You are reading with expression and your mom is giving you supportive praise."

This observation of parents and children working together is a crucial part of the workshop in terms of supporting reading progress. You can oversee the strategies that are being used.

- Is the parent allowing enough wait time?

- Does the parent encourage the reader with specific praise?

- When the child is stuck on an unfamiliar word, is the parent giving suitable prompts to encourage the child to figure out his or her mistakes independently?

- Are the parent-child teams discussing the story together?

Using the information collected while observing allows you to direct other meetings if you believe some aspect of the workshops needs clarification. You can repeat the Buddy Reading Station as often as you like in your own classroom during the school day. You can also invite a few parents at a time into your room to listen to their child read. This would give you another opportunity to coach parents who might be having difficulty being as supportive as necessary. Our school district invites parent into classrooms during American Education Week. This is an excellent time to practice adult-child reading.

Station 2: Reading Activities and Games

Our goal with this station is for students and parents to enrich vocabulary and enjoy practicing phonics together. The facilitator distributes the same game to each parent-child team. Often, two teams will decide to play together. Each color-coded group participates in different games.

Periodically throughout the year, children are sent home with an activity or game to support whatever skill is being learned in class. These games are meant to reinforce a skill that has already been learned in school, not for parents to teach something new. The advantage of an activity or game is that the child is likely to play it more than once with parents and siblings. This provides them with additional reinforcement rather than a one-time worksheet. We suggest activities be played at home at least once with adult participation, adult supervision, or both, to be sure the directions are understood and the skill is actually being practiced correctly. We prefer activities to games early in the school year as there does not have to be a winner. Some children with poor self-esteem are hesitant to participate in games if they believe they are being tested. Sometimes, too, the parent feels that the child must win all the time and fakes losing, when the activity should be fun for the whole family.

In our reading programs, we engage students actively in the reading process daily. The reality is that finding 5 minutes at the end of a lesson to play a game can be a significant reward for a child. It may be the promise of a game that gets them through the daily struggle they engage in with reading. The games are not only educational but enjoyable, which is a beneficial combination for children. When brought home, these activities offer the parents a chance to work on reading skills in a relaxed manner. This adds to the rapport they have been trying to build with their child.

At the end of this chapter you will see three sample games we use in our workshops (Figures 5.6 through 5.8). We change these games every year so they are new. The appropriateness of these games can be adapted for the beginning to more advanced reader by changing vocabulary or phonetic element. You can use these games or create some of your own. There are many valuable resources available in teacher stores or catalogs. We find the

Figure 5.6. Rhyme Time Activity

Directions: Place your playing piece on start. Roll one die and move that many spaces. Parent and child teams read the word they land on aloud and give one rhyming word. More advanced players can find a rhyme and use one of the words in a sentence.

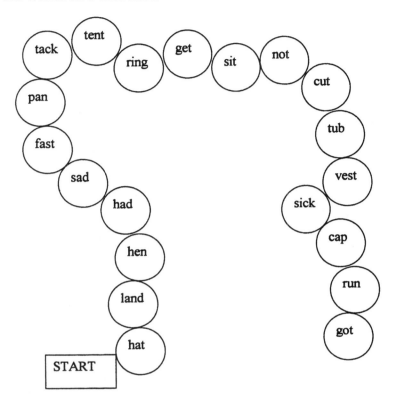

most successful games have easily understood directions, clearly identifiable skills, and offer some adaptability as to how they are played. The game boards and simplified directions should be reproducible so that children can take them home to remind them of the fun they had at the workshops.

Station 3: Interactive Writing Response

The purpose of this station is to observe parents and children engaging in an interactive writing project. We demonstrate how literature serves as a model for good writing.

The facilitator reads a story book with an open-ended theme that both the children and the adults can easily relate to. Throughout the reading, the facilitator models fluent, expressive reading. After the story is read, each parent-child team is asked write a story together, using the book as a

Figure 5.7. Sight Word Roundup Activity

Facilitator preparations: Materials needed include the following:

1. Find 20 to 30 high-frequency sight words that you are working on with your group. You can use curriculum related words for children at higher levels.
2. Write each word on an index card.
3. Have ready one die for each parent-child team.

Game directions:

1. Place the sight word cards on a table face up.
2. The first player rolls the die and reads that number of word cards. If the word is read correctly, the player keeps the card. If the word is not known, it should be read correctly by someone else and is left on the table.
3. Play continues until all the cards have been read correctly.

---

springboard for ideas. The group spends a few minutes brainstorming ideas for writing. The facilitator then distributes premade blank writing booklets that the parent and child can use together. These booklets can be taken home to be completed and used as a reminder for good writing.

Because this is an example of interactive writing, parents can work with their child to write a response together. Parents can guide their child, sometimes modeling and sometimes asking for their child's input. Parents should help where needed and use exact spelling. Throughout the session the facilitator circulates, observing and providing positive input and suggestions for improvement.

> "Rena, it's wonderful the way you and your mother are working together breaking that longer word down into syllables, figuring out how to spell it correctly."

> "Mark, you and your Dad really have a unique idea. You did a great job rereading your writing to check if your ideas are clear. Did you reread to check your punctuation?"

Near the end of the station time, the children proudly share their writing with the facilitator or other parent-child teams. If time allows, students could present their stories to their group.

Figure 5.8. Riddle Concentration Activity

Purpose: To match the riddle with the beginning blend or digraph of the response.

Facilitator preparation: Use the cards below or create a set of your own. The set should include a number of riddle cards and a matching set of blend and digraph cards. The blend/digraph cards should be the beginning sounds of the riddle answer.

Game directions:

1. Place all the cards face down on the table.
2. Player one turns over two cards. In order to make a match, the blend/ digraph card must represent the beginning sound of the riddle's answer. If there is a match, the player keeps the two cards. If there is no match, the cards get returned to their face-down position in the same place.
3. Play continues until all cards have been picked up.

What do you do with a glass of milk?	dr
Where do birds build their nests?	tr
What do lightning bugs do?	gl
What can you ride down the hill in the winter?	sl
What number comes between two and four?	thr

Agenda for Workshop 4

1. Get ready for summer reading by:
   - Suggesting a leveled book list
   - Discussing fun ideas for extending stories
   - Promoting local library and bookstores summer reading programs
   - Maintaining a summer reading log
2. Children present skits, plays, poems, murals, and book readings they have created related to the reading process
3. Present participation certificates
4. Have refreshments

The fourth workshop is planned to celebrate the year's success of parents and children working together in the reading and writing process. We want to extend through summer the bond that has grown between parent and child by encouraging them to continue to work together.

This workshop has a dual agenda. We first discuss summer reading plans and instill an expectation that reading is becoming a lifelong leisure activity. A list of suggested books for reading is distributed in our summer reading packet (see Figure 5.9). The books are leveled so parents and students can use this as a guide. Parents find it helpful if we provide them with their child's reading level as of the end of the school year. After having read a few books, parents can extend the list by using the book selection techniques from their resource guide.

Also included in the summer packet is a log where children can list the books they have read. There are also suggestions for fun ways to respond to literature.

It is helpful to investigate local summer readings programs through libraries and bookstores and share the information with parents. One idea is to invite the librarian to the workshop to give a brief description of the themes and incentives involved in the program.

The second portion of the workshop is the grand finale. All children are involved in some capacity in the evening's production. All materials for the children's presentations require preparation. The fact that we have multiple facilitators definitely helps, and you can adjust your program accordingly. Our program opens with everybody participating in a choral reading of a poem. Children at the emergent stages of development prepare a poster that titled "What I like to read about!" using a combination of text and illustrations. At the workshop, children present their individual work to the audience by reading what they have written.

The rest of the students are divided into small groups. Each group responds to a story they have read during the year. Groups present plays, commercials, or raps. Earlier in the week, children create modest costumes and scenery that enhance their shows. The audience genuinely appreciates the entertainment, and the workshop ends with good feelings all around.

Our four workshops are based on information we wanted to share with parents to help them become more effective reading partners. The overall philosophy of the workshops, that of positively developing independence in readers, applies to all children.

You will need to define the purpose of your workshops, keeping in mind the needs of your student population, what their parents need to know, and the goals you hope to accomplish. Chapter 6 provides answers to some of the questions we have been asked about adapting workshops to individual situations. Remember to keep your agenda flexible for unexpected parental concerns.

Figure 5.9.   "Book Pals" Summer Reading Packet

Enjoy your vacation!

My Summer Reading Log

I promise to read _____ minutes each week.

Child's signature _____

Parent's signature _____

Reading Log: _____

_____

_____

_____

_____

_____

_____

_____

_____

_____

_____

_____

_____

_____

_____

_____

_____

_____

_____

Glass, L., Peist, L., & Pike, B. *Read! Read! Read!: Training Effective Reading Partners.*
©2000. Corwin Press, Inc.

Figure 5.9. Continued

Fun Things to Do to Extend
the Reading Experience

1. Make a poster of your favorite book.

2. Write a letter to a relative about something you have done this summer.

3. Cut 15 happy words out of the newspaper.

4. On separate pages, draw pictures of family members and tell a story about each one of them.

5. Make paper bag puppets. Give a puppet show to a friend.

6. Make edible fingerpaints: 2T instant clear gelatin, 1/4 cup sugar, 1 pack unsweetened Kool Aid, and 3/4 cup water. Mix together. Illustrate one part of your favorite book.

7. Read a riddle book. Make up some riddles yourself.

8. Keep a journal and write in it every day.

9. Write color names across a page. Under each one, list things that are that color.

10. Look at magazines and cut out the longest word you find, the funniest word, the saddest word, the smallest word, and so forth.

11. Write and illustrate a book about your pet.

12. Visit the library and take out a book by a favorite author.

13. Draw a picture of each room in your house. Label the furniture in it.

14. Make creative clay: Mix 2 cups flour with 1 cup salt. Mix with enough water to form "dough." Store it in an airtight container. Sculpt your favorite character.

15. Make an ABC book. Cut out pictures for each letter and paste it on separate pages.

16. Buddy read with your friends.

17. Make three columns on a sheet of paper. Title each column People, Places, and Things. Cut out pictures and glue them under the proper heading. These are nouns.

18. Read a fairy tale together. Use a different voice for each character.

Glass, L., Peist, L., & Pike, B. *Read! Read! Read!: Training Effective Reading Partners.* ©2000. Corwin Press, Inc.

Leveled Book List for Summer Reading

Level	Title	Author
6	*Bears on Wheels*	Berenstain, Stan and Jan
6	*Crabapple*	Reese, Bob
6	*Dirty Larry*	Rookie Reader
6	*Ice Is—Whee!*	Rookie Reader
6	*Mary Wore Her Red Dress*	Peek, Marie
6	*Paul the Pitcher*	Rookie Reader
6	*Too Many Balloons*	Rookie Reader
7	*It Looked Like Spilt Milk*	Shaw, Charles
8	*The Blanket*	Burningham, John
8	*Ear Book*	Perkins, Al
8	*Eat Your Peas Louise*	Rookie Reader
8	*Foot Book*	Dr. Seuss
8	*Herman the Helper*	Kraus, Robert
8	*Inside Outside Upside-Down*	Berenstain, Stan and Jan
8	*Nose Book*	Perkins, Al
8	*Where Can It Be?*	Jonas, Ann
9	*Are You There, Bear?*	Maris, Ron
9	*Harry Is a Scaredy Cat*	Barton, Byron
9	*Huzzard Buzzard*	Reese, Bob
9	*Is Anyone Home?*	Maris, Ron
9	*Just Like Daddy*	Asch, Frank
9	*Rosie's Walk*	Hutchins, Pat
10	*Cars*	Rockwell, Ann
10	*Cookie's Week*	Ward, C., and de Paola, T.
10	*Dark Dark Tale*	Brown, Ruth
10	*Harry Takes a Bath*	Ziefert, Harriet
10	*Marmalade's Nap*	Wheeler, Cindy
11	*Boats*	Rockwell, Ann
11	*Cat and Dog*	Minarik, E. H.
11	*Critter Race*	Reese, Bob
11	*Dinosaurs, Dinosaurs*	Barton, Byron
11	*Just for You*	Mayer, Mercer
11	*Sheep in a Jeep*	Shaw, Nancy
12	*The Big, Fat Worm*	VanLaan, Nancy
12	*Boris Bad Enough*	Kraus, Robert
12	*Carrot Seed*	Krauss, Ruth
12	*Jason's Bus Ride*	Ziefert, Harriet
12	*Mine's the Best*	Bonsall, Crosby
12	*Why Can't I Fly*	Gelman, Rita
13	*The Awful Mess*	Rockwell, Anne
13	*Buzz, Buzz, Buzz*	Barton, Byron
13	*Danny and the Dinosaur*	Hoff, Syd
13	*The Rabbit*	Burningham, John
14	*Animal Tricks*	Wildsmith, Brian
14	*Building a House*	Barton, Byron
14	*What Game Should We Play?*	Hutchins, Pat

Figure 5.9. Continued

Leveled Book List for Summer Reading

Level	Title	Author
15	*Great Day for Up*	Dr. Seuss
15	*Green Eggs and Ham*	Dr. Seuss
15	*Just a Mess*	Mayer, Mercer
15	*Messy Bessy*	Rookie Reader
16	*Angus and the Cat*	Flack, Marorie
16	*Just Me and My Dad*	Mayer, Mercer
16	*Kiss for Little Bear*	Minarik, E. H.
16	*Noisy Nora*	Hutchins, Pat
16	*Trucks*	Rockwell, Anne
17	*Ask Mr. Bear*	Flack, Marjorie
17	*The Doorbell Rang*	Hutchins, Pat
17	*Hand, Hand, Fingers Thumb*	Perkins, Al
17	*Let's Be Enemies*	Udry, Janice
17	*Mouse Soup*	Lobel, Arnold
18	*Clifford the Big Red Dog*	Bridwell, Norman
18	*Curious George* (series)	Rey, M.
18	*Little Bear*	Minarik, E. H.
18	*More Tales of Oliver Pig*	VanLeeuwen, Jean
19	*Frog and Toad* (series)	Lobel, Arnold
19	*Mr. Gumpy's Outing*	Burningham, John
19	*Surprise Party*	Hutchins, Pat
20	*Arthur* (series)	Hoban, Lilian
20	*Bony-Legs*	Cole, Joanna
20	*Caps for Sale*	Slobodkina, Esphyr
20	*Case of Cat's Meow*	Bonsall, Crosby
20	*Madeline*	Bemelmans, L.
20	*Nate The Great* (series)	Weinman, Sharmat
20	*Whistle for Willie*	Keats, Ezra Jack
20	*The Wind Blew*	Hutchins, Pat
20-25	*Cam Jansen* (series)	Adler, David
20-25	*George and Martha*	Marshall, James
20-25	*Junie B. Jones* (series)	Park, Barbara
20-25	*Pee Wee Scouts* (series)	Delton, Judie
20-25	*Pinky and Rex* (series)	Howe, James
25-30	*Bailey School Kids* (series)	Dadley & Jones
25-30	*A Chair for My Mother*	Williams, Vera
25-30	*Freckle Juice*	Blume, Judy
25-30	*Jenny Archer* (series)	Conford, Ellen
25-30	*Polk Street Kids* (series)	Reilly Giff, P.
25-30	*Russel Rides Again*	Hurwitz, Joanna
25-30	*Spy on Third Base*	Christopher, Matt

Facilitating Your 6
Own Workshops

I n Chapter 5, we provided you with our model for organizing parent and parent-child workshops. Information in this chapter will help educators who are interested in facilitating workshops. We have found the increased parental support to be very valuable for our struggling readers, and we hope you will find it just as worthwhile. These workshops can be held for any group of parents who you are expecting to become engaged in working with readers and writers.

Following are some basic questions that facilitators should consider before making the commitment to lead the workshops. Answering them will allow you to organize your thoughts and clarify your goals.

- How will holding parent workshops benefit my students?
- What do I want the parents who attend the workshops to learn?
- What information should I know to facilitate workshops?
- Do I have building administrator support?
- Who will attend the workshops?
- How many workshops will I hold?
- How much time can I allot to these workshops?
- When is the best time to hold the workshops so that I maximize parental participation?
- Where will I hold the workshops?
- Are there any colleagues who will facilitate these workshops with me?
- Will I be compensated for running these workshops after school hours?

Now that you have answered these questions, you have set some realistic goals for yourself. You have decided what information and techniques should be shared with parents and how to enlist their assistance in their children's reading progress.

Even though the focus of the workshop is being determined by you, it is helpful to talk with colleagues about your purposes. These workshops can be even more successful when the facilitator is able to enlist the support of other colleagues or administrators. As support teachers, we have found it beneficial to make classroom teachers aware of our workshops. We held a brief inservice for the teachers in our school, explaining the components of the workshops and shared our parent resource guide with them. This fostered a feeling of cooperation throughout the school and established a common sense of purpose. This helped in our discussions with parents at the workshops because we knew the teachers were using similar techniques in their classrooms.

Overall Questions and Answers About Conducting Workshops

Who Can Lead the Workshops?

Actually, anyone who works with children learning to read and has a sound foundation about what makes good readers can facilitate a workshop. Reading specialists, resource room teachers, classroom teachers, librarians, district reading supervisors, Reading Recovery™ teachers, Title I teachers, building administrators, or any combination are all potential candidates to facilitate workshops. The most important qualities of the facilitator are knowledge of the subject matter, desire to include parents in the reading process, and flexibility in addressing parental concerns. If at all possible, including a colleague in the workshops can be really helpful. They can share in the work and offer a strength you may not possess. Another person can relieve any tension or nervousness you may feel about talking in front of a large group. They also can provide insights that may have escaped your notice.

Which Group of Parents Should I Invite to the Workshops?

As you look at your students, you need to consider who would most benefit from parental involvement. You will probably answer, "all of them," and that is definitely true. If your students' reading abilities are close in developmental stages, you could probably meet with all of the parents. However, if you have a group that is struggling with reading, it is perhaps those parents you should target. You do not need to limit yourself to inviting just the students you work with. If you are comfortable expanding your target audience and you are in a position to do so, you may want to extend invitations to parents whose children you do not directly teach.

Another idea might be to invite all parents to the first workshop to introduce them to your program and let them know how you need their support in helping their children to become more independent in their use of strategies. Subsequent workshops could be for parents of those children who have not yet succeeded in making the reading connection or have specific weaknesses. The options are endless and you can try as many combinations as you wish. The most important thing is that you get started.

What Do These Parents Need to Know to More Effectively Help Their Children?

We believe the most important concept to convey to parents is the need for a positive, supportive learning environment at home. This is especially true of parents working with struggling readers. Having them relax and learn how to enjoy the time spent with their children is an important breakthrough.

Parents require an understanding of the developmental nature of reading and where their children fit in the total spectrum. They need to know what to look for as evidence of their children's learning. Sometimes this includes vocabulary building, reading strategies for figuring out words, watching student writing, and using specific strategies for questioning techniques and improving comprehension.

Once parents understand that their children will learn to read in time, frustration is diminished and children receive more positive support. If you want the parents to be listening to their children read aloud, be sure to discuss the good reading buddy behaviors located in the parent resource guide at the back of this book. Parents must be made to understand that readers need to be given adequate wait time, which allows them to have the opportunity to self-correct.

Parents should also be encouraged to follow any reading with a conversation about the text. Questioning techniques that promote higher-level thinking skills are vital for parents to receive. Too often parents get caught up in word recognition and need to realize the importance of comprehension.

How Important Is Parent Feedback?

The parent questionnaire in Chapter 5 is an extremely important link between the facilitators and the parents. It provides credibility with the parents, developing trust that you are actually trying to engage them in the reading process with their children. The questionnaire should be taken home, filled out, and returned to the facilitator. This way parents have time to reflect on what they learned at the workshops, implement some of the techniques, and think about what else they would like to know. Each group of parents has a slightly unique set of concerns. Our workshops have been altered after we have received the surveys and noticed common parental concerns, so be open to their questions, answering them as honestly as you can, and do not be afraid to change your plan if different needs arise.

How Many Parents Should I Invite?

We have found parents representing up to as many as 40 children is a manageable number, but with a group that large, you may want to have more than one facilitator. Remember that the number of bodies more than doubles at the parent-child workshops. Any group that is larger than that loses the closeness you are trying to create. This is especially true if you are working with parents whose children are having a particularly difficult time in learning to read. There are issues that parents may want to discuss, but they may feel awkward talking in front of too large a group.

Our first year we started by inviting small numbers of parents to allow ourselves to become comfortable with the content of our program. As time went on, we became better at inviting and encouraging more parents to attend. We opened up the workshops to parents of other students in the school as it became easier to speak to larger groups. If your first-year turnout is rather small, do not be discouraged. We hold the philosophy that if even a few parents attend and receive our message, then we have made a difference.

How Can I Encourage Parents to Attend the Workshops?

First of all, do not give up the project if you do not get an overwhelming response. It is important for the parents who did show up and their children to get your continued support. Attendance will improve once the parents who participated in the workshops start talking about it. Many parents need to know that this program is different than other meetings they have attended. They should be made aware that at the workshops they will not just be talked at or have unrealistic expectations placed on them. Instead, they will learn practical techniques that enable them to become actively engaged in their children's literacy. One way to convey this message is at Back to School Night, which usually happens within the first few weeks of school. We briefly explain our program and personally invite the parents to attend. It also helps to continually send flyers, make phone calls, and write articles for your school or local newspapers describing the program.

If parents have a lack of transportation or no baby-sitter, we provide them with a list of suggestions. In the past, neighbors have offered to carpool and our school social worker has driven parents. Baby-sitting services can be provided, possibly using high school student volunteers or grant money. Students can also be a catalyst for parental attendance, and you can build excitement for the program through them. If the children want to attend, often they will encourage the parents to participate.

How Can I Assist Parents Who Have Limited Literacy or Speak English as a Second Language?

All parents should be invited to attend the workshops. You can encourage those parents who have difficulty with English or reading to bring a translator, older child, or a neighbor to assist. If this is a large-scale concern, you will want to give directions and information simply, avoiding educational jargon. You can use charts and diagrams to help clarify your presentation. When a child comes home with a book to reread, parents can listen as the child reads to a neighbor or talks into a tape recorder. Children could bring in the tape for the educator to listen at his or her convenience for additional support. It would be beneficial to send home some appropriately leveled multicultural text when available.

Who Else Can Be Trained to Assist the Program?

Sometimes parents, for a variety of reasons, are not the people who assist their children with homework. Grandparents, guardians, older siblings, or caregivers are also invited to attend our workshops. If children attend a before- or afterschool program where homework is completed, the supervising adult can also be made aware of the program. Our goal is to reach one or more individuals in each child's life who will offer consistent support in reading.

There are many volunteers outside the school staff who are willing to help children with their reading. These include senior citizens, high school and college students, student teachers, and any adult willing to participate as a volunteer. Our belief is that although they can be a good source of help, volunteer tutors must be properly trained by the facilitator to be effective in the schools. They should be instructed in the same material parents receive during the first two workshops. This should be done early in the school year before they begin working with the children.

What Details Must Be Taken Care of Before Each Workshop?

Now you must think about some of the housekeeping chores for holding the workshops. When selecting dates for the workshops, make sure they do not interfere with other planned school activities. Ideally, the first two workshops should occur as early in the year as possible. We send home books to be reread as soon as school begins, and we want to get information to parents as soon as possible. This allows them to start monitoring their children's rereading in a positive and effective manner. The second workshop should take place approximately 1 month after the first, allowing parents time to implement at home what they have learned. This also gives them time to determine if they have any questions or concerns that need to be addressed at the second workshop. Other things to consider include purchasing and setting out the refreshments, alerting the custodial staff of your workshop so that the workshop room will be available and chairs will be set up, and sending out invitations.

Would a Demonstration Video Be an Effective Tool?

A video made of our students' reading really brings to life what we are talking about at the workshops. We tape a sampling of children at different stages of reading ability: emergent, transitional, and expanding. Each segment lasts only about 3 to 5 minutes. We emphasize the positive interaction that takes place between the reader and the adult. Samples of prompts, praises, and questioning are demonstrated. We stop the video between segments to discuss what has occurred and what strategies have been used. It is a good idea to have parents sign a release giving permission to video their children.

How Do I Adapt the Workshops in Future Years?

If your workshops include multiple grade levels of students there is a good chance you will have parents who could attend for more than 1 year. Although this needs to be addressed, it is not a major concern. The input we have received from parents repeating the workshops is that although they are aware of the information, hearing it again allows them to use techniques more automatically. In addition, their children move along the continuum, and parents have new concepts to learn as we offer different information.

What Happens if a Parent Misses the First Workshop of the Year?

The first workshop of the year is the foundation for the entire program. The information disseminated there provides the basic components parents need to be effective reading partners. If they miss this workshop, it is crucial that they be given an opportunity to make it up. One way to handle this problem is to encourage parents to attend the second workshop 30 minutes early. At this time parents can be given brief summaries that emphasize the important points made at the first workshop. The parent resource guide can be distributed and explained. The videotape that was shown at the first workshop can be made available on loan.

Organizing Parent-Child Workshops

These workshops are usually the ones that receive the most inquiries. The best advice that we can offer is to be prepared and keep the parent-child workshops fast-paced, hands-on, and manageable. Whereas the parent meetings may have been accomplished without much difficulty, adding youngsters to the mix changes the tone in addition to more than doubling the number of people. These workshops are entertaining and educational but require more organization and preparation.

How Can I Adapt the Station Workshops to My Needs?

These stations are a way for the facilitators to see how much the information disseminated at the earlier parents-only workshops is being put to practical use. If you are not working with other staff members and need to lead all the stations by yourself, you will need to prioritize and hold the stations at different times. The stations could be separated and presented on different days, or you could conduct the stations with all the parent-child pairs consecutively, rather than simultaneously, and keep the activities shorter. Perhaps you could arrange for someone to assist you, not to direct the meetings, but to act as another pair of trained hands. Sometimes a parent from a previous year or a building administrator may volunteer to attend and assist you. If you are a classroom teacher, you might enlist the help of the basic skills reading teacher, resource teacher, or Title I teacher.

Which Stations Should I Use?

You should analyze the needs of your students to decide which activities you should use as stations. You may have students who have more trouble engaging in reading, so you might want to focus on book selection, the buddy reading station, or both. If the audience consists of children who are already reading strategically, you might want to concentrate on the reading/writing station or the game station to practice reading skills.

If the population you are working with consists of parents who have English as a second language or limited literacy, you may want to create a station that addresses their special needs. This could take the form of a demonstration station where the facilitator offers step-by-step instructions in basic literacy activities. This could include showing how to use books on tape and a more simplified version of buddy reading.

How Much Time Should I Allocate for the Workshops?

We allot about 20 minutes for each station. If time is an issue, workshops could be briefer or you may have only one station. Remember to choose your activities according to your specific needs. You could invite a few parents at a time and have the stations during your regular class time. You could also stagger the evening times and have a smaller group of parents and children for a more condensed amount of time. If the students are at the same developmental stage, you can have the parents attend together. The goal is to decide how much you can handle successfully and then focus on whatever aspect of the workshop you have chosen.

How Will I Know How Many Participants to Plan For?

Although we ask our parents to RSVP, not all of them do. We have learned to be prepared. Have all your materials ready and include extras. There is always someone who drops in unexpectedly because plans change and they become available. We have had siblings of our students attend (although they were not invited) and have included them in the activities if they were age appropriate. We also create extra materials just in case more people show up.

What Do I Do With People Who Arrive Early?

The parents are usually content to sit and converse with other parents or the facilitators before the meeting. We found that having an activity for the students ahead of time is helpful. We created an activity packet for the children to work on that included mazes, coloring pages, reading inventories, word puzzles, and so forth. Because the children who attend our workshops are in grades 1 through 3, we try to provide an array of activities with differing developmental levels so there is something for everyone.

What Kinds of Games and Activities Should I Use at Workshop 3?

It is best to stick with your old favorites, those activities and games that you know work well with children. Try to make sure that it is a game that this particular group of children has not yet played. They like to be surprised with something new. Keep the directions short and clear. It can be noisy, and there are both children and adults who are not good listeners. Have two games planned for each 20-minute session. As in any teaching situation, it pays to overplan.

At the end of Chapter 3 we included a list of resources for games. Create a bank of games to share with parents to foster skill development. Keep adding to it so that each year you have fresh ideas but are able to refer to previous games in subsequent years. You might want to share some of your ideas with colleagues at your same grade level in exchange for activities their students enjoy.

What Incentives Could I Use for the Parent-Child Workshops?

If you choose to give prizes, all children should be rewarded. The incentives should be based on attendance, not performance. We distribute incentives at each station at Workshop 3: pencils at the reading/writing station, bookmarks at the reading buddy station, and foam dice and minierasers used as game pieces at the game station.

As an additional incentive we provide refreshments at the end of all the workshops. They are more elaborate at the last two workshops when the children are invited. The treats should be simple finger foods that will not cause a mess, such as juice boxes and ice cream cups. Your parent organization may be willing to sponsor the snacks.

We have provided you with information to run your own workshops. Getting started is the most difficult part. The rewards are worth the added effort and will supplement your reading program in a truly positive way. Flexibility, openness, knowledge, and organization are key factors to remember when facilitating the workshops. (If you have additional concerns, you can e-mail us at **Book Pals@aol.com**.)

Students Who Need More Support

Although most children meet success with the techniques used in our reading program, there is a segment of the school population that requires extra support. In our teaching experiences, we have all encountered students who, no matter how hard they try, still experience trouble learning. These children may have hidden problems that affect their ability to read and write. It is a challenge for the educator to be creative and individualize instruction to meet the needs of these children.

Children who have an especially difficult time learning to read may have one or more of a variety of problems. One part of the population consists of children coming from homes where parents are either non-English speaking or have low literacy skills. Some of their parents attend our workshops but are still unable to provide enough support at home even though they are eager to help. For children who are struggling with literacy due to this lack of support at home, additional educational opportunities need to be provided.

Other children may learn at a slower rate or have a learning disability. Although they may show growth in other areas, they have difficulty expressing thoughts in writing, gaining meaning from reading, or simply learning letters, sounds, and words. Some children are strong visual or tactile learners, whereas others learn best through their auditory channel. If, however, children are weak in more than one of these areas, they usually have the most difficult time learning to read. We offer suggested ways parents and teachers can provide support for these children using a *multi-modality* approach. When children are learning they should be able to see, hear, and touch the materials, giving them a better chance of absorbing the skills.

We find that these groups of children benefit from integrating additional activities and techniques with those being taught at the workshops. In all cases, early intervention is critical. Often, the window of opportunity in which to help these students is limited. The earlier children can be helped, the better their chance of success. For children needing extra support, we usually recommend these additional techniques at individual conferences, as most children do not need that much reinforcement.

These children often feel inadequate, comparing themselves with their peers. As children are struggling to learn a difficult task, it is imperative that parents create a positive, stress-free environment, celebrating children's successes even when they come in small steps. Efforts must be made to make reading a more pleasurable and successful experience. We encourage parents to give extra attention to developing self-esteem and confidence by accentuating the strengths of their children.

We have organized this chapter to reflect the most typical reading and writing problems primary children encounter. Before we recommend any interventions, we suggest to parents that they have their children's vision and hearing checked. This will eliminate the possibility of a physical problem that may be affecting their children's ability to learn.

Multimodality—Using more than one of the five senses simultaneously.

Children Who Do Not Know All Letters of the Alphabet

Lack of letter knowledge affects children's ability to read and write successfully. We work with struggling beginning readers who cannot identify all of their letters and spend time ensuring that the letters are learned. However, we begin reading instruction simultaneously as the learner engages in letter activities. We believe that children can begin developing a sight vocabulary without knowing all the letters.

Interventions to Support Letter Recognition

It is important for children to be able to play with letter shapes whether they are forming them using *tactile/kinesthetic* materials or they are premade by an adult. These activities incorporate children's entire bodies to maximize their learning potential. A touch-tray can be made from a cookie sheet with approximately an inch of sand, salt, or powdered gelatin in it. This can be used to write letters free-form or copy them from a model. Children can use a write-on bag to practice forming letters correctly. A write-on bag is made by putting two tablespoons of bright colored finger-paint into a resealable plastic bag. The bag is reinforced on all four sides with heavy-duty duct tape. Children use their finger to push on the bag

Tactile/Kinestetic—Activities that involve the sense of touch.

Figure 7.1. Recipe for Pretzel Dough

1. Preheat oven to 425 degrees.
2. Mix the following ingredients together in a large bowl: 1 package yeast, 1 1/2 cups water, 1 tablespoon sugar, and 1 tablespoon salt.
3. Add 4 cups of flour.
4. Knead the dough on a floured surface until it is smooth.
5. Shape the dough into letter shapes.
6. Bake in the oven for 15 minutes until brown.

while practicing writing their letters. The write-on bag is used like magic slates. Pretzel dough (see Figure 7.1) can be formed into the shape of letters, baked, and then eaten. Modeling clay can be used for the same purpose. Adults can cut letters out of rough sandpaper and the children can go over them with their fingers. The goal is to provide as many opportunities as possible for children to see, feel, and even taste the letters. Children are learning while they are having fun.

The following are letter interventions to remember:

- Touch-tray for tracing and writing letters
- Write-on paint bag
- Form pretzel dough or clay into the shape of letters

Children Who Have Difficulty With Left-to-Right Directionality When Reading and Writing

Children who have trouble tracking print with their eyes may have a visual-perception weakness. This problem causes the eyes to shift, affecting a child's ability to keep his or her place when reading. Reading then slows down and meaning can be lost. Visual difficulties also manifest themselves in writing. These children cannot copy from the board or overhead projector. Their writing is uneven and does not start from the beginning of each line.

Interventions to Improve Left-to-Right Directionality

These children will need to use a finger for tracking purposes longer than others who are learning to read. Once they can visually scan a line of print when reading, the finger can be placed at the beginning of each sentence to act as a marker for them to follow. Another device for tracking is called a window box. Teachers take an index card and cut a square in the middle of it that will fit one word. The child moves the card along the book as they read each word that appears in the window. It may be necessary to cut the index card horizontally in half to make it easier to control.

Sentence strips are an excellent tool for children to use. After reading, a sentence is copied from the book and the teacher cuts it up into individual words. Children are instructed to piece the sentence back together in the correct order, which reinforces left-to-right directionality.

When writing, the teacher needs to decide what children are capable of independently. It helps if a child's paper has dark lines that are easy to distinguish. The teacher can mark the beginning of each line with a green dot so the child knows that is where they begin writing. If work has to be copied off the board, they should be allowed to move up as close as possible. If children take too long to copy the material, a piece of carbon paper can be given to another child who can make a copy as they write. If the teacher uses certain phrases routinely, such as days of the week or headings, those words can be written on oak tag and laminated to be placed near the child's desk for easier copying.

The following are directionality interventions to remember:

- Finger for tracking print

- Window box made out of an index card

- Sentence strips

- Paper with darkened lines and green dots

- Close proximity when copying work

- Peer assistance

Children Who Have Difficulty Remembering Sight Words

We often hear parents state that their children say a basic sight word such as *and* or *the* correctly on one page and do not remember it on the next. Even after the parent reinforces the word several times, children continue to substitute another word or forget the word entirely. This can lead to an enormous amount of stress on the part of parents who cannot understand why their children are unable to remember what they perceive as a simple word. Children can sense this tension, which can cause them to associate negative feelings with reading.

There are several possible reasons why children have difficulty with word recognition. They may have a problem with their memory that interferes with the word being retained. Although they see the word multiple times, it fails to become part of their permanent bank of instantly recognized words. Another possibility is that their *visual perception* may be weak. They might easily confuse words with similar configurations such as *tag* and *tap* or *where* and *were*.

Without the ability to have a permanent bank of reading sight words, children must stop at each word and try to figure out what it says. This is difficult, especially with high-frequency words that are not phonetically regular. This causes reading to become very tedious and destroys any meaning they need to get from the text.

Visual perception—
Ability to visually extract information from the people, places, and things around us.

Sight-Word Interventions

There are many games and activities that can be used to support the acquisition of a sight-word vocabulary. The most important of these is reading appropriate literature daily, reinforcing word recognition in context. Another technique is to send a group of sight words home on flashcards that children should practice repeatedly or use in game formats. These should be high-frequency words taken from the children's reading. For some children, another modality needs to be added for flashcards to meet with success. To enhance the flashcard technique, put glue and colored sand on each letter and use the look, say, and touch method. When children are learning a new word they look at it while tracing their fingers over the sand, spelling and saying it aloud. This gives the word a chance to enter the memory through auditory, visual, and tactile learning channels. These flashcards can be sent home so parents can reinforce this method with their children each day. We have found that the beginning reader should receive a limited number of new words a week. It is important to allow time for children to learn these words before sending new ones home.

Once children receive new words, they should have as many opportunities as possible to use them during the day. The words should be placed in a personal dictionary that contains only the sight words they have learned. The dictionary can be made of paper stapled together or a composition notebook that leaves room for a picture next to the word. The picture can act as a visual clue to help children remember the word. Although some sight words lend themselves to easy picture representations such as house or dog, others are harder to create. The word *and*, for instance, is difficult to represent in picture form. However, children could draw or cut out pictures from a magazine of one person standing next to another that shows "mommy *and* daddy." Although this may sound abstract, the fact that they have created the picture means that the word has a better chance of being retained. This dictionary should be kept in an accessible place for children to refer to when needed.

Children can also use pictures to create *mnemonic devices*. A mnemonic device is a picture or phrase that helps an individual to remember. In the sight word *look*, for example, the *os* can be made into eyes that trigger a memory of the word. These devices can be used for letter recognition, spelling, and memorizing facts.

For children who are experiencing difficulty retaining sight words, spelling assignments should be adapted by the teacher. Having to complete spelling activities using sight words as well as studying them for a weekly test extends children's exposure to these words. If a classroom program is being used that is inappropriate for the struggling student, there are published sight-word spelling materials specifically designed for this purpose.

Tactile activities can be used to provide additional practice. Adults can provide shaving cream, whipped cream, or even chocolate pudding to smear on a placemat, cookie sheet, or table. Children then write the new words into the cream as another method of reinforcement. They can also practice writing the words in the air, on someone's back, or on the palm of their own hand with their finger.

Another item teachers can use is highlighting tape to help children locate a sight word in context. Highlighting tape is transparent colored tape that adheres to books and papers temporarily, and can be pulled off and reused again. In any activity that requires reading, children can be responsible for finding and highlighting their sight words. Because the words being learned are the most frequent in the English language, there are many opportunities to find them.

Sight-word games offer an entertaining way for children to learn their words. Concentration can be made from two sets of identical word cards. In this game, children need to remember and locate the matching word pairs. These same word cards can be used to play the game Go Fish. Each player is dealt the same number of word cards to keep in their hand with the remaining cards placed in the center of the table face down. The object of the game is to collect as many word pairs as possible. Teachers can also create a simple bingo board using children's sight words.

The idea is to try and reinforce the words in as many ways as possible using these multimodality techniques. This builds on children's strengths and maximizes learning potential.

The following are sight-word interventions to remember:

- Limiting the number of sight words introduced each week
- Tactile flashcards
- Personal dictionaries
- Mnemonic devices

Mnemonic device—A picture or phrase that helps the memory.

- Integration of sight words in spelling program
- Shaving cream, whipped cream, chocolate pudding, and so forth
- Writing in the air, on someone's back, or on their palm
- Highlighting tape
- Sight-word games

Children Who Have Letter and Word Reversals

A common concern among parents is that their children reverse letters and words when reading and writing. For some children this is a developmental behavior that they will outgrow. If children continue to reverse letters and words, then they may have a problem that requires additional support.

Learning how letters and words fit into the universe is a very difficult concept. Until the first time children are exposed to letters, objects in their world remain constant. A cat is a cat no matter how it is presented, whether it is upside down, running, or sitting still. When introduced to letters, children are shown an object that changes meaning depending on where it is spatially. The letter /m/ only stays an /m/ if the bumps are placed on the top. Flip the letter upside down, putting the bumps on the bottom, and the /m/ becomes a /w/. Turn /m/ on its sides and it becomes the number three or the letter /E/. The same is true for words such as *was* and *saw*, which many children reverse.

Interventions for Letter Reversals

As with the other interventions, the goal is to provide as much multimodality help as possible to address the reversal problem. Children with letter reversals should have an alphabet strip placed on their desk at school and at home to use as a reference. Children should be encouraged to check with the strip as needed. Educators can laminate portable letter cards with the troublesome letters on them to be carried around for fast reference when children are not at their seats. The letters should be underlined to provide correct spatial orientation. The use of primary lined paper with regular or raised lines helps support the positioning of the letters.

Tactile activities can be used to help children learn the correct way the letters should be formed. Wikki Stix, a flexible, thin material similar to pipe cleaners is very good for this process. The stix can be bent into the shape of any letter by children and then touched as they say the letter name. As with other problems, glue and sand, shaving cream, whipped cream, and chocolate pudding can be used as a tactile method to reinforce the correct letter or word formation.

Either before or after reading a book, children can "hunt" in the text for the letters they reverse and place highlighting tape over them. This technique can also be used for word reversals. For instance, if children confuse *was* and *saw*, having them highlight the first letter of the word draws their attention to it when reading.

Because reversals also appear in writing, crayons or colored pencils are a good tool. When children are receiving writing instruction, the teacher models the proper formation of a letter using two colors. In the letter /b/, the line would be drawn with one color while the ball would be drawn in another color. This provides children with a visual representation and another key for remembering.

The following are word reversal interventions to remember:

- Place alphabet strip on desk
- Portable letter cards
- Tactile activities
- Highlighting tape
- Crayons and colored pencils for writing instruction

Children Who Have Poor Phonics Skills

Many struggling readers exhibit weak phonemic awareness and have a difficult time linking letters with their sounds. There are several reasons why this may occur. Children may have learned to read by using a sight-word method or have not had direct instruction in phonics. They could have been taught phonics in isolation and are unsure of how to apply the generalizations in the context of reading. It is possible, too, that an individual might not be developmentally ready or lacks the phonemic awareness to hear the sounds adequately. If these reasons are the cause, then with direct phonics instruction, children should be able to learn and apply letter sounds and phonetic rules.

If, however, children experience a weak auditory channel, learning phonics may be extremely difficult for them. This problem may prevent them from discriminating between letter sounds. Although it is still important to try and remediate this problem, the educator should make parents aware that some children cannot learn to apply all the phonetic sounds and generalizations when reading. All children must be encouraged to use a variety of other strategies to help them figure out unknown words.

Interventions for Phonics Knowledge

Children with poor phonics skills need to be instructed using an organized, sequenced phonics program that is an integral part of their total reading program. At the workshops, we teach parents of beginning readers to look for a chunk or part of the word they may know instead of trying to sound out each letter. For example, the word *sat* has the /at/ chunk in it, and children should figure out the word if they recognize this chunk and the beginning sound of /s/.

There are many ways to develop an understanding of these chunks to make words. One way is by creating a list of rhyming words from the chunks and sending it home for practice. On the list, colored pencils or sand and glue are used to distinguish the chunk from the rest of the word. This way children are learning not only the vowel sound but also a strategy to help them break apart and figure out an unknown word.

Teachers also use magnetic alphabet letters in which the consonants and vowels are different colors. Metal objects like cookie sheets are used as a work surface to form words with the same chunk. We also teach children to identify a chunk by first having them learn all the rhyming chunks in the same family. Using each chunk, we create a rhyming rap on a tape that is sent home with children. They find the words on their list while they hear it on the tape. This provides visual and auditory reinforcement.

A flip book can be created in which the chunk stays the same but the initial consonant sound is flipped over changing the word. Children can also use highlighting tape after reading and place it on the chunk part of the word found in the book.

The following are phonics interventions to remember:

- Color-coded rhyming chunks
- Rhyming rap on tape
- Phonics flip book
- Highlighting tape

Children Who Have Poor Reading Comprehension

Comprehension is the purpose for reading. Readers manifest comprehension difficulties in different ways. There are children who read so slowly that by the time they get to the end of the page they have no idea what has been read. In contrast, some children read fluently yet also show no understanding of the stories content. Fluency is not an indicator of how much children are comprehending, and assessment is needed to check understanding. There are also children who have difficulty getting literal or inferential meaning from what they have read.

Interventions to Improve Comprehension

One of the primary reasons children experience difficulty understanding what they have read is due to reading material that is too difficult. Careful selection of appropriate-leveled literature is vital to the success children have when reading. Books should be chosen using the 1-in-10 or five-finger rule. The use of high-interest, low-readability books encourages weaker readers to become involved in stories appropriate for their age and interest. Stories that can be read easily and hold children's interest have a better chance of being understood.

One strategy children with comprehension difficulties can learn is to read the story more than once. Rereading allows more opportunities to understand the information. This is especially advantageous for children who have fluency problems. As they reread, they recognize words more readily, allowing them to focus on the content of the story.

Parents can provide additional support for comprehension as they read aloud to their children and discuss the books they have read. Children can also listen to stories on tape. Most libraries have extensive collections that can be borrowed. Sometimes parents like to tape their own stories so their children can listen to them in the car or when they are not together. They could also enlist other family members to tape stories about family history or amusing anecdotes. These activities allow children to focus on story content as opposed to word recognition, maximizing the opportunity to comprehend story meaning. As children develop, they can use the taped books independently to follow along, reinforcing both auditory and visual input.

Sometimes it is difficult for children to understand larger portions of a book, especially when they first begin to read chapter books. The book can be broken up into manageable parts by periodically responding to the text. Readers can do this by jotting important ideas or questions on Post-it™ notes while reading. Referring back to these points after the book is finished helps the child remember and better understand what has been read. It also teaches children to question themselves and monitor their thinking while they are reading.

When working with content-area material, children frequently have difficulty identifying important facts under a major heading. Highlighting tape placed over key points under each heading works in a similar manner as the Post-it™. The goal is to help children organize information while they are reading rather than waiting until the end when there is too much information to remember.

For children struggling with comprehension, a story map can offer them a visual frame of reference. Story maps come in many forms and usually ask the reader to describe the setting, problems, important events, and solutions. This helps organize factual information in a systematic manner, allowing them to then respond to more open-ended inference questions. A story map is only one example of the many graphic organizers that can be used to help children visualize what is happening.

The following are comprehension interventions to remember:

- Reading appropriately leveled literature
- Rereading a story
- Literature on tapes or having parents read aloud
- Post-it notes™ and highlighting tape for noting key points
- Story maps

Children Who Come From Homes Where Parents Have Low Literacy Skills or Speak a Foreign Language Exclusively

There are children whose parents are unable to provide assistance at home because they may not speak or read English at a sufficient level to offer reading support. These children are at greater risk because there is limited support for literacy learning. Although their parents want them to succeed, they do not have the tools necessary to help. There are some solutions to this problem that do not require a lot of extra time and effort by the teacher.

Interventions to Support Parents With Low Literacy or English as a Second Language

Children from these homes require additional support from school. They need to be given opportunities to read individually to adults or older children. Many schools districts have local high school student or adult volunteers participate in a one-on-one tutoring program. These individuals would need to be trained in using the appropriate reading techniques and should be invited to the first two workshops. This help would be supplemental to children's regular support programs and would not replace instruction from their teachers. Teachers of children with foreign language backgrounds could work closely with their English-as-a-second language teacher for more support and coordination of the curriculum and reading techniques. To develop vocabulary, these students could work on puzzles or picture cards with their classmates. The children could also be buddied up with capable classmates who can provide some additional reading support. These children should be reminded of using positive buddy reading techniques, including supportive praise.

At home, these children can read aloud to a relative or neighbor who might be willing to accompany the parents to the workshops. The children could also read aloud into a tape recorder, and their teacher could listen to it the next day. Listening to prerecorded stories or watching videotapes would provide them with additional literacy experiences.

The following are interventions to remember:

- Enlisting help from other trained adults
- Peer tutoring
- Using a tape recorder
- Listening to stories on tape

Although most children meet success with the techniques taught at the workshops, some need additional support to succeed. The earlier these interventions begin, the more likely these children are to develop independent reading skills and maintain their self-esteem. We have found that reinforcing concepts with a multimodality approach integrated into the reading program gives these children the best chance of learning.

Source for Activities

Goodman, G. (1995). *I can learn! Strategies and activities for gray-area children.* Peterborough, NH: Crystal Springs Books.

Parent Resource Guide

A Note to Educators: Using the Parent Resource Guide

The parent resource guide is intended to support the workshops. It summarizes the major points of the program and provides parents with concrete suggestions to use at home. There are a variety of ways for facilitators to help parents attain the maximum benefit from this guide. Ideally, this guide should be distributed during the first two parent workshops. This is where it can be explained, and parents are afforded the opportunity to have their questions clarified.

This guide was formatted to be adapted for your individual needs to be used in its entirety or in segments. We discuss and distribute the sections from "Creating a Positive Learning Environment" to "Using Specific Praise" at the first workshop. Use what you need to support your program. The guide focuses on the following points:

- Creating a positive learning environment
- Using the developmental reading ladder
- Selecting appropriate books
- Being a good listener
- Prompting the reader
- Using specific praise
- Guiding comprehension
- Using the developmental writing ladder

Glass, L., Peist, L., & Pike, B. *Read! Read! Read!: Training Effective Reading Partners.* ©2000. Corwin Press, Inc.

Book Pals' Parent Resource Guide
Helping Children Experience Reading Success

Striving To Succeed

B ecoming an independent reader

O pening hearts & minds to reading

O bserving reading & writing strategies

K nowing you have a special place to read

P raising builds self-esteem & confidence

A ccelerating reading progress

L earning to love reading

S haring special parent-child reading time

Glass, L., Peist, L., & Pike, B. *Read! Read! Read!: Training Effective Reading Partners.* ©2000. Corwin Press, Inc.

Welcome to Book Pals!

An Overview

Book Pals is a program designed to help struggling readers achieve success through the cooperation of parents and educators. You play an integral part in this process. By investing your time in reading this resource guide and attending as many of the workshops as you can, you are making a commitment to help your children succeed in reading.

We realize that many of today's families no longer fit the traditional model, and often in this busy world parents are not the only ones to help with schoolwork. We use the term *parents* to include grandparents, guardians, caregivers, homeschoolers, or any adult who supervises children's reading. We applaud the efforts of anyone who helps support children's journeys into the world of literacy.

Our goal is to empower your children to take control of their own reading. We want them to become confident, independent readers. We teach children to use a variety of strategies to figure out unfamiliar words and handle text when the meaning is not clear. Strategies are thoughts that readers use to figure out words while getting meaning from the text. We are providing your children with tools they need to make them independent readers.

However, until your children are independently monitoring their own reading, adult listeners will need to provide assistance to remind readers to use different strategies. This is where parents and educators must work hand in hand to develop proficiency as well as make reading enjoyable. Your children will be bringing home books to reread to you that we have already read in class. Rereading at the early stages helps to reinforce sight vocabulary, practice reading strategies, and increase fluency and comprehension. We can accelerate progress with positive practice. As your children's reading abilities strengthen, you will notice them accepting more of the responsibility for their reading.

Glass, L., Peist, L., & Pike, B. *Read! Read! Read!: Training Effective Reading Partners.* ©2000. Corwin Press, Inc.

You must realize that the use of strategies does not happen all at once. On the following pages, we have put together a developmental reading ladder of strategies as they change with time. Though they are presented sequentially, children acquire them at their own pace.

Children can develop strategies best when they read appropriately leveled material. This means using books that are not too hard or too easy. Children cannot use strategies effectively if they are reading material that has too many words that they cannot instantly recognize. We expect your children to be reading material that offers them a challenge, but at a level where they are able to maintain control over the text.

Throughout this resource guide we will provide you with enough information and techniques to use to help you assist your children improve their reading. Educators and parents should work as a team. This guide is important because children benefit from a consistency of techniques used in both school and home. We will share with you what your children are learning to do for themselves at school and how you can provide positive support. We focus on:

- How to create a supportive home environment
- How children develop strategies along the reading ladder
- Frequently asked questions that reflect common parental concerns
- How children can select appropriate books to read
- How children can figure out words they do not know
- How to use prompts to encourage independence
- How specific praise can be beneficial
- Strategies used by good comprehenders throughout the reading process
- How to have conversations about stories
- How children develop strategies through the writing stages

Parents, remember that your child's classroom teachers are valuable sources of information on your child's progress. Keep in close contact with teachers as you help your child learn to read. If you feel your child is struggling with the reading process and are unsure as to what to do, we recommend that you arrange for a parent-teacher conference.

Creating a Supportive Learning Environment

It is crucial when helping children learn that we set a positive and supportive environment at school and at home. Children must feel that their efforts are respected and that they are encouraged to take risks without fear of embarrassment or punishment.

We make several recommendations for you to use when working with your children.

- Set aside a special time and quiet place for the two of you to read. Parents may want to share with each other the responsibility for helping their children.

- Have reasonable expectations. Each child develops at a different pace and you must allow for individual differences. Children should not be compared with siblings, relatives, or neighbors.

- Provide an atmosphere that encourages risk taking. Do not overcorrect your children's reading. Praise their efforts even if they are incorrect. Realize that reading does not have to be perfect to be meaningful.

- Promote independence by allowing sufficient wait time for your children when they are unsure of a word or meaning. Wait a few seconds to give them a chance to make corrections before you offer prompts. If you help too early, you could be weakening your child's self-confidence. They will believe that they can only be successful through the efforts of others and are incapable of fixing their own mistakes.

- Emphasize what your children can do by using specific praise for thoughtful attempts. Confidence is a very powerful motivator. All children need to see themselves as successful readers.

The Developmental Reading Ladder: Steps to Reading Success

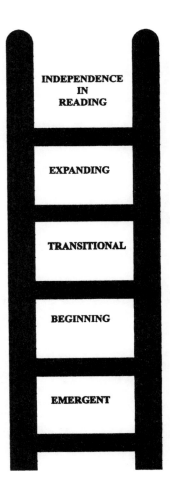

From the time your children were young and you read to them, they have been learning about books and literacy. They have heard stories and know that ideas can be written down. Children understand that when reading, they turn pages, and that illustrations make the stories come alive. As they learn to read, they will come to know more about books and language. Your children will need you to provide support, praise, and patience as they progress toward independence, eventually learning to successfully monitor their own reading. They will build an ever-increasing bank of sight words and will acquire, over time, a set of strategies that will help them learn to figure out new words and get meaning from print.

Glass, L., Peist, L., & Pike, B. *Read! Read! Read!: Training Effective Reading Partners.* ©2000. Corwin Press, Inc.

Strategies are thoughts that readers use to get meaning from text and to figure out unknown words. Below is a list of strategies in approximately the sequence in which readers develop them. Not all children will use every strategy listed. You can help them accelerate their growth by prompting them to use these strategies. Eventually, children are expected to use these strategies independently.

The following information on developmental stages gives you an awareness of the strategies your children are expected to use at each step. If they bring home a Level 3, check with the list to find out what strategies a Level 3 reader is expected to use. If you are unsure of your children's reading level, then check with their teacher.

Emergent Stage: Book Levels 1 Through 4

1. Children understand that reading is meaningful, not random words. They make a connection between oral language and what is written down.

2. Children are able to follow with their finger from left to right across the page.

3. Children should point their finger at each individual word showing they understand what a word is.

4. Children use pictures as the primary clues to help them figure out a word and to predict what is happening.

5. Children focus on the beginning consonant of a word to help them read.

6. Children start to accumulate a bank of words recognized by sight. As reading levels increase, so does the number of words known automatically.

7. Children attempt to read fluently and with expression. (This never changes throughout the levels. Children may slow down to attempt a difficult word, but fluency resumes as soon as possible.)

Parents can

- Read the book aloud before having their children read it to them
- Make their reading sound like talking to model good expression
- Hold their child's hand to make sure he or she is pointing to each word
- Discuss the pictures to reinforce the story
- Reinforce unknown letter sounds by making a letter book with magazine pictures

Beginning Stage: Book Levels 5 Through 8

1. Children use strategies from all previous book levels.

2. Children can identify words that rhyme. If they read, "the cat is on the mat," they can tell you that *cat* and *mat* rhyme.

3. Children check their prediction of what they thought might happen to see if it makes sense.

4. Children demonstrate an awareness of ending marks (!, ?, .) when reading orally.

5. Children begin to reread from the beginning of the sentence to help determine an unknown word or if something does not make sense.

6. Children start to read to the end of a sentence using meaning to help figure out an unknown word.

7. Children check the beginning and the ending consonant of a word while reading.

8. Children identify known "chunks" in a word (e.g., /ick/, /ing/, /an/).

Parents can

- Draw their children's attention back to the print if they appear to be looking elsewhere

- Read rhyming books and have their children identify the rhymes to support knowledge of chunks

- Praise their children's use of reading strategies

Transitional Stage: Book Levels 9 Through 13

1. Children use strategies from all previous book levels.

2. Children identify and begin to apply known blends and digraphs in unknown words (e.g., /st/, /bl/, /gr/, /ch/, /sh/).

3. Children can take a rhyming chunk and apply it to an unknown word.

4. Children begin to notice and apply word endings (e.g., -ing, -ed, -er, -s)

5. Children look at the word from beginning to end to apply all phonetic skills learned to date.

6. Children stop periodically to think about the story and summarize important events.

Parents can

- Use magnetic letters to practice making words in which you hear every sound—for example, they can use the /at/ chunk and have their children make words such as bat, flat, brat, cat, chat, and splat
- Make word lists with their children of harder rhyming chunks such as /ill/, /atch/, /end/, and /ump/
- Discuss the story with their children, asking questions that require more thought
- Praise their children's use of reading strategies

Expanding Stage: Book Levels 14 Through 20

1. Children use strategies from all previous book levels.
2. Children extend their knowledge of vowel patterns to include long vowels, r-controlled vowels, and variant vowels in one syllable and multisyllabic words.
3. Children use strategies to search for clues in pictures and words, check for meaning, and self-correct what does not make sense.
4. Children do not give up but try every possible strategy they know before they ask for help.
5. Fluency is adjusted by children depending on the type of material being read. With a new book, a strategic reader may slow down for a short moment to read a difficult new word, then resume reading fluently.
6. When discussing the story, children concentrate on the author's message using details to support conclusions made.
7. Children begin to read easy chapter books. They spend more time reading silently and using their strategies independently.

Parents can

- Praise children for trying a variety of strategies and not giving up
- Encourage more silent reading from their children
- Have conversations about the books their children are reading
- Provide access to different types of books for their children to read
- Help children decide how many syllables they hear in a word by having them tap a finger on a table for each syllable. Some children find it easier to place their outstretched hand under their chin as they say the word. Each time their chin touches their hand they count it as a syllable. Understanding syllables aids in reading and spelling longer words.

When readers become independent they are able to use many strategies for figuring out words.

If the word still does not make sense, I can get help from another reader.

As children progress beyond Level 20, they increase the time they spend reading silently and assume most of the responsibility for their reading. They are more likely to read books for pleasure, as reading has become easier for them. Children begin to read more difficult chapter books, expanding their vocabulary. Readers are learning about contractions, compound words, homonyms, suffixes, and prefixes. This knowledge enables them to figure out more unknown words. With their expanded abilities, parents should provide an opportunity for children to read a variety of poems, mysteries, biographies, fiction, and nonfiction.

Frequently Asked Questions

Parental concerns are understandable when trying to help children learn to read. Children are taught to use a variety of strategies that place them in control of their own reading, and these strategies change as they progress. When parents are able to place their children on the developmental reading ladder, it helps them realize that many of the reading behaviors that have caused concern are only temporary. Listed below are frequently asked questions from parents concerning their children's reading.

My son has memorized the text and is not really reading the words. What should I do? Often, children at the earliest stages will have a short book memorized and will run their finger along the words, not matching what they have said with the word at which they are pointing. These children have not yet developed the one-to-one correspondence of matching each word with what they are saying. At this stage, students should be asked to point to each word as they read. We often need to take their finger in our hand and help them point to each word as they reread the text. This is a technique that parents can use at home.

Should I cover the pictures to make sure my child is really reading? Parents should not cover the pictures. Children are taught to use pictures as one strategy in figuring out unfamiliar words. Let your children use the pictures as a guide. The need to depend on pictures will lessen as children become better readers and are able to rely more on the text. Parents will also notice that as the number of words on a page increases, pictures become less helpful to the reader.

Why isn't my child sounding out words? Phonics is developmental, and children learn to use these skills in a sequential order. Your daughter may not be ready at this time to apply all of the phonics she will learn. The

Glass, L., Peist, L., & Pike, B. *Read! Read! Read!: Training Effective Reading Partners.* ©2000. Corwin Press, Inc.

reading ladder will provide you with appropriate phonics for her current book level.

How come my child can read a word on one page and not on another? The fact that many words in the English language do not look like they sound make them difficult for young children to learn. There are words that we call sight words including *of, two, the,* and *would* that children will eventually have to memorize because of their uniqueness. These words can often be read by children in the context of a whole sentence but not in isolation. At other times, some sentences provide more support for word recognition than others. Regardless, it simply indicates that that particular word is not really known by your child. We encourage the growth of sight vocabulary by having children read and reread books on their level.

Why is my son moving up levels, and yet he does not seem to be using any of the strategies you talk about? Some children are able to begin to read by relying on their sight vocabulary. However, without strategies children are limited to reading only words that they already know. Your son's teacher moved him up a book level where he will encounter some unknown words, forcing him to apply strategies. As listeners we must reinforce these strategies by using prompts.

Selecting Appropriate Books

Sometimes teachers select books to be used in class for a guided reading lesson, and at other times children are given an opportunity to pick books themselves. Children are taught to choose books that are on an appropriate level for them, using the indicators listed in the next section.

If your children are interested in reading a text that is too difficult, you can read it aloud to them. Children of all ages benefit when adults read to them. They develop good listening skills and are exposed to more complex language structures than they would be able to handle themselves at this time. When sharing nonfiction, children also gain new concepts and vocabulary. You and your children can talk about the stories you read, which will improve comprehension and stretch their thinking skills.

Children may also pick books that appear too easy for them. This is acceptable at times because easier text allows children to practice reading fluently. They are also able to focus on the meaning when they are not struggling to decode the text. However, children should be encouraged to challenge themselves and read books on their appropriate level.

Techniques for Selecting Books

For Book Levels 1 through 4, parents can select a few appropriately leveled books and then allow their children to pick a book from the group that they wish to read.

For Book Levels 5 through 12, you might find the 1-in10 rule to be more suitable. Children should not make more than 1 error in every 10 words they read if the book is at an appropriate level.

The five-finger rule (for Book Levels 13 and above):

1. Readers should open up the book they want to try and read any one page.

2. They can count the words that they cannot figure out by themselves.

3. If there are more than 5 words they do not know, the book might be too difficult.

4. If they still want to read that book, someone older can read it to them.

Being a Good Listener

As you are listening to your children read, they will meet some words that are unfamiliar to them. An immediate reaction is to tell them the unknown word. However, this solution usually gives readers the message that they are incapable of figuring out the word themselves, and they will come to rely on others rather than themselves for corrections.

Buddy Reading

A good listener will . . .

1. Pay attention to the reader at all times

2. Give readers time to fix their own mistakes

3. Fix only those mistakes that interfere with meaning. If a child substitutes a word that does not change the overall meaning of the story, ignore it and let them keep reading.

4. Give hints about using strategies. Remind readers to do the following:
   - Look for picture clues
   - Use beginning sounds
   - Use rhyming chunks
   - Read from the beginning of the sentence
   - Read to the end of the sentence

Glass, L., Peist, L., & Pike, B. *Read! Read! Read!: Training Effective Reading Partners.* ©2000. Corwin Press, Inc.

5. Offer help when asked

6. Praise the reader's efforts

7. Discuss the story with the reader

Prompting the Reader

Prompts are questions you ask to encourage your child's taking control of his or her own reading. You are directing your child's attention to recall strategies he or she can use to help figure out unknown words or to clear up confusion about the meaning of what is being read. This process takes time and patience. Please work with your child in the supportive manner that we have discussed.

Below are some suggested prompts you can use when listening to children read to help them become more independent.

Word Prompts

The following questions can be used when your child is stuck on a word. Remember to wait a reasonable amount of time to give readers time to figure it out on their own.

- Can you get any clues from the picture?
- Why don't you start again at the beginning of the sentence?
- Can you read the rest of the sentence and then go back to the word?
- Look at the beginning sound. What word would make sense here?
- Does the word you said look like the word on the page?

Meaning Prompts

Sometimes children begin to encounter difficulty with reading because the story has stopped making sense. Readers may need to stop and reread a section of the story to take control of the meaning. They may need to stop and think about the story and discuss it. You can use these questions when your children guess at a word that does not make sense.

- Does what you are reading make sense?
- What is happening in the story?
- What do you think will happen next? Why do you think that?

Glass, L., Peist, L., & Pike, B. *Read! Read! Read!: Training Effective Reading Partners.* ©2000. Corwin Press, Inc.

Strategic Awareness Prompts

Eventually, children gain control of their reading and are able to use strategies for themselves. You may want to check to see what strategies they are using to monitor their reading.

- It looks like you are stuck on that word. What can you do to help yourself figure out that word?
- I like the way you knew that word in that sentence. What did you do to help yourself figure it out?
- Why did you stop reading? How can you figure out what is going on in the story?

Using Specific Praise

Of all the techniques and concepts that you use to help your children succeed, none are more important than praise. Children who are struggling with reading often have low self-esteem and self-confidence. They often feel so overwhelmed they do not want to try. By offering a few words of encouragement, you can convey to your child that you have confidence in his or her ability to become a successful reader.

Although general positive encouragement is appreciated, it is best to be specific in praising the strategies your child is using. Vague phrases such as, "You did such a good job," do not tend to support your child's reading development. The phrases suggested on the next page offer more specific praise. By being more exact in what you say, you are reinforcing the strategies your child is using and he or she will more likely repeat the correct reading strategies again. Specific praise may take a little practice, but it goes hand in hand with offering prompts. Remember to praise your child for using strategies independently without having to be reminded by you.

Praise Phrases

I like the way you . . .

- Looked at the first letter of the word
- Used the picture as a clue for that word
- Found a chunk that you knew in the word
- Used your finger to point at each word
- Checked to see if what you were reading made sense
- Went back to the beginning of the sentence and read it again so it sounded more like talking
- Did not give up when you got stuck on that word
- Looked at the book and not at me for help

Glass, L., Peist, L., & Pike, B. *Read! Read! Read!: Training Effective Reading Partners.* ©2000. Corwin Press, Inc.

Guiding Comprehension

Teachers instruct students to monitor the meaning of what they are reading before, during, and after the story. During guided reading lessons, teachers demonstrate strategies to improve comprehension and provide students with opportunities to try these strategies. Teachers also listen to children read individually and discuss stories with them. Efforts to encourage children to relate to stories are made from the earliest levels. Children develop the ability to deal with meaning, just as they progressed in figuring out unfamiliar words.

Following are strategies that children will learn to use when they are confused about what the author means. You can help by prompting them with questions, just as you did when they were stuck on a word.

Strategies Good Comprehenders Use

Before reading, readers should:

- Predict: They should think about what might happen in the story by using pictures, the title, their own experiences, or prior knowledge. (If their prediction is not the same as the author's, it can be acceptable if it is based on information from the story.)

During reading, readers should do the following:

- Question themselves as they read
- Monitor their own reading by going back if something they read did not make sense
- Visualize what the author describes by picturing it in their heads
- Change predictions as the author adds new information
- Think about how characters feel or try to understand why they acting a certain way
- Figure out unknown words. When they are stuck on an unknown word, use picture clues, beginning sounds, word chunks, and sentence meaning to read it

After reading, readers should do the following:

- Summarize the story to themselves or share it with a friend. They can think about the beginning, middle, and end using their own words.

Glass, L., Peist, L., & Pike, B. *Read! Read! Read!: Training Effective Reading Partners.* ©2000. Corwin Press, Inc.

- Think about the whole story. What was it really about? What message do they think the author was trying to tell?

- Personalize the story by relating it to any experiences they have had or another book they have read.

Sharing a Story

After your children finish reading stories aloud or silently, you should take some time to discuss what they have read. When stories are shared, children have the opportunity to think about the text, the author's message, and make it meaningful to their own life experiences. It should be a carefree time that can spark children's imagination and foster a love of reading. Story discussions should not seem like an interrogation so children feel they are being tested. The ultimate goal is for children and adults to engage in conversations about books on an equal footing. All participants should be responsible for asking questions and sharing their reactions and thoughts. Know that this may take several years, but you should see your children taking increasing responsibility for getting meaning from the text.

Listed below are suggestions that will help you encourage your children's comprehension through story conversations.

Establish a comfortable setting. The discussion should be brief and more like a conversation. Remember to praise your children's efforts in taking risks or thinking of original ideas.

Have children summarize the story aloud in their own words. They can reflect on the meaning of the story as they recall important events sequentially and relate them to personal experiences.

Some children may need additional prompts. If your children are having difficulty understanding the story, you may need to ask a few questions. Try to avoid too many factual questions. It is most important that your children make inferences, including drawing conclusions or making judgments rather than simply recalling the text. The author gives clues, but the reader needs to figure out what they mean. Be open to your children's efforts. Remember they have limited experiences so their responses may be different than yours but just as acceptable. As long as their answer makes sense and relies on information from the text, it should be positively acknowledged.

Share your ideas about the story. After your children have expressed what they think, it is beneficial to share your thoughts, especially if they are different from your children's ideas. The two of you can brainstorm other

Glass, L., Peist, L., & Pike, B. *Read! Read! Read!: Training Effective Reading Partners.* ©2000. Corwin Press, Inc.

responses, using information from the book and realizing that there can be more than one acceptable answer. This is also a chance to enrich your child's vocabulary by introducing new words in context.

Check with your children's teachers if you have concerns. Comprehension is the key to reading. The teachers can share with you how your children are doing in class.

The Developmental Writing Stages: Steps to Writing Success

Children begin to understand that written words will help them convey a message. As they learn to recognize more sight words and gain control over sound-symbol relationships, their writing and spelling strengthens. The messages they write will become longer, using more complex language. They will apply more conventional spellings and learn to use strategies to help them spell unfamiliar words. As students progress, they will become better at using proofreading strategies independently. As adults we need to patiently support writers, encouraging them to take risks by experimenting with language. Children should be given real-life opportunities. They can write postcards, letters, journals, grocery lists, and stories.

Stage 1

Early writers will do the following:

- Begin experimenting with writing by scribbling
- Sometimes draw pictures to show what they want to communicate
- Randomly string letters together in an attempt to tell a story
- Talk about their stories and try to retell them

Parents can do the following:

- Encourage children to write and draw often
- Write a story that children dictate to them modeling left-to-right directionality, spacing, and correct spelling

Glass, L., Peist, L., & Pike, B. *Read! Read! Read!: Training Effective Reading Partners.* ©2000. Corwin Press, Inc.

- Read their children's message aloud with them
- Rewrite children's independently written messages using correct spelling underneath the original writing

Stage 2

As children develop, they can do the following:

- Begin to match letters to their corresponding sounds
- Use beginning and ending consonant sounds to spell words
- Begin to put a space between words
- Usually omit vowels in words
- Know that writing goes from left to right

Parents can do the following to help:

- Darken the margin line so children will know to start writing each line on the left side of the page
- Continue to occasionally write stories children dictate
- Remind children to put one finger space between each word
- Review children's writing to help correct some beginning and ending consonant sounds
- Overemphasize the letter sounds when correcting spelling

Stage 3

By this stage, writers are able to do the following:

- Create short readable sentences
- Add a medial vowel in the right place, but not always the correct one
- Interchange upper- and lowercase letters
- Experiment with capitalization and punctuation
- Spell some words correctly and use phonics to write others independently

Parents can do the following:

- Expand children's writing by asking questions to encourage them to write more

Glass, L., Peist, L., & Pike, B. *Read! Read! Read!: Training Effective Reading Partners.* ©2000. Corwin Press, Inc.

- Offer support when their children are correcting consonants and medial vowels in spelling
- Praise capitalization and punctuation efforts and help fix some of these mistakes

Stage 4

As progress continues, writers will do the following:

- Learn the conventional spelling of many more words
- Organize ideas into a beginning, middle, and end
- Use medial vowels more accurately
- Use capitals and endmarks regularly
- Correctly spell word endings (-ing, -ed, -s, -es)

Parents can do the following to help:

- Encourage children to take risks in their writing and explore topics they have not previously written about
- Discuss the organization of a story to be sure the order makes sense
- Check that previously learned spelling words are spelled correctly

Stage 5

Ultimately, writers will be able to do the following:

- Recognize when a word is spelled incorrectly. They will experiment with alternate spellings and check with the dictionary or other writers to confirm that it is correct
- Write longer, more complex sentences
- Become more responsible for independently revising and editing their own work

Parents can do the following:

- Encourage children to proofread before asking for help
- Read their children's work and praise the good qualities in their writing

A Final Note to Parents

Thank you for participating in the workshops. We are confident that the time you have invested will positively influence your child's literacy success. We applaud your commitment and hope you and your child now find reading to be a pleasurable experience. The lessons you have learned will be valuable throughout your child's educational career, enabling you to be an integral part of his or her learning. Even though children become more independent in their reading, they will always benefit from your continued support as it fosters their self-esteem and confidence. The special bond you have developed when reading together and the trust you have built will last a lifetime.

Index

CORWIN
PRESS

The Corwin Press logo—a raven striding across an open book—represents the happy union of courage and learning. We are a professional-level publisher of books and journals for K–12 educators, and we are committed to creating and providing resources that embody these qualities. Corwin's motto is "Success for All Learners."